This Book has be

Publishing Date: 2005

ISBN# 1-59547-984-8

Please see our website for several e-books created for education, research and entertainment.

Most eBooks are available in paperback.

Specializing in rare, out-of-print books still in demand.

Contact: sales@nuvisionpublications.com

URL: http://www.nuvisionpublications.com

AN ACCOUNT OF EGYPT

By: Herodotus

Translated By G. C. Macaulay

Table of Contents

CHAPTER 1

When Cyrus had brought his life to an end, Cambyses received the royal power in succession, being the son of Cyrus and of Cassandane the daughter of Pharnaspes, for whose death, which came about before his own, Cyrus had made great mourning himself and also had proclaimed to all those over whom he bore rule that they should make mourning for her: Cambyses, I say, being the son of this woman and of Cyrus, regarded the Ionians and Aiolians as slaves inherited from his father; and he proceeded to march an army against Egypt, taking with him as helpers not only other nations of which he was ruler, but also those of the Hellenes over whom he had power besides.

Now the Egyptians, before the time when Psammetichos became king over them, were wont to suppose that they had come into being first of all men; but since the time when Psammetichos having become king desired to know what men had come into being first, they suppose that the Phrygians came into being before themselves, but they themselves before all other men. Now Psammetichos, when he was not able by inquiry to find out any means of knowing who had come into being first of all men, contrived a device of the following kind:--Taking two new- born children belonging to persons of the common sort he gave them to a shepherd to bring up at the place where his flocks were, with a manner of bringing up such as I shall say, charging him namely that no man should utter any word in their presence, and that they should be placed by themselves in a room where none might come, and at the proper time he should bring them she-goats, and when he had satisfied them with milk he should do for them whatever else was needed. These things Psammetichos did and gave him this charge wishing to hear what word the children would let break forth first after they had ceased from wailings without sense. And accordingly it came to pass; for after a space of two years had gone by, during which the shepherd went on acting so, at length, when he opened the door and entered, both children fell before him in entreaty and uttered the word *bekos*, stretching forth their hands. At first when he heard this the shepherd kept silence; but since this word was often repeated, as he visited them constantly and attended to them, at last he declared the matter to his master, and at his command he brought the children before his face. Then Psammetichos having himself also heard it, began to inquire what nation of men named anything *bekos*, and inquiring he found that the Phrygians had this name for bread. In this manner and guided by an indication such as this, the Egyptians were brought to allow that the Phrygians were a more ancient people than themselves. That so it came to pass I heard from the priests of that Hephaistos who dwells at Memphis; but the Hellenes relate, besides many other idle tales, that Psammetichos cut out the tongues of certain women and then caused the children to live with these women.

7

With regard then to the rearing of the children they related so much as I have said: and I heard also other things at Memphis when I had speech with the priests of Hephaistos. Moreover I visited both Thebes and Heliopolis for this very cause, namely because I wished to know whether the priests at these places would agree in their accounts with those at Memphis; for the men of Heliopolis are said to be the most learned in records of the Egyptians. Those of their narrations which I heard with regard to the gods I am not earnest to relate in full, but I shall name them only because I consider that all men are equally ignorant of these matters: and whatever things of them I may record I shall record only because I am compelled by the course of the story. But as to those matters which concern men, the priests agreed with one another in saying that the Egyptians were the first of all men on earth to find out the course of the year, having divided the seasons into twelve parts to make up the whole; and this they said they found out from the stars: and they reckon to this extent more wisely than the Hellenes, as it seems to me, inasmuch as the Hellenes throw in an intercalated month every other year, to make the seasons right, whereas the Egyptians, reckoning the twelve months at thirty days each, bring in also every year five days beyond number, and thus the circle of their season is completed and comes round to the same point whence it set out. They said moreover that the Egyptians were the first who brought into use appellations for the twelve gods and the Hellenes took up the use from them; and that they were the first who assigned altars and images and temples to the gods, and who engraved figures on stones; and with regard to the greater number of these things they showed me by actual facts that they had happened so. They said also that the first man who became king of Egypt was Min; and that in his time all Egypt except the district of Thebes was a swamp, and none of the regions were then above water which now lie below the lake of Moiris, to which lake it is a voyage of seven days up the river from the sea: and I thought that they said well about the land; for it is manifest in truth even to a person who has not heard it beforehand but has only seen, at least if he have understanding, that the Egypt to which the Hellenes come in ships is a land which has been won by the Egyptians as an addition, and that it is a gift of the river: moreover the regions which lie above this lake also for a distance of three days' sail, about which they did not go on to say anything of this kind, are nevertheless another instance of the same thing: for the nature of the land of Egypt is as follows:--First when you are still approaching it in a ship and are distant a day's run from the land, if you let down a sounding-line you will bring up mud and you will find yourself in eleven fathoms. This then so far shows that there is a silting forward of the land. Then secondly, as to Egypt itself, the extent of it along the sea is sixty *schoines*, according to our definition of Egypt as extending from the Gulf of Plinthine to the Serbonian lake, along which stretches Mount Casion; from this lake then the sixty *schoines* are reckoned: for those of men who are poor in land have their country measured by fathoms, those who are less poor by furlongs, those who have much land by parasangs, and those who have land in very great abundance by *schoines*: now the parasang is equal to thirty furlongs, and each *schoine*, which is an Egyptian measure, is equal to sixty furlongs. So there would be an extent of three thousand six hundred furlongs for the coast-land of Egypt. From thence and as far as Heliopolis inland Egypt is broad, and the land is all flat and without springs of water and formed of mud: and the road as one goes inland from the sea to Heliopolis is about the same in length as that which leads from the altar of the twelve gods at Athens to Pisa and the temple of Olympian Zeus: reckoning up you would find the difference very small by which these roads fail of being equal in length, not more indeed than fifteen furlongs; for the road from Athens to Pisa wants fifteen furlongs of being fifteen hundred, while the road to Heliopolis from the sea reaches that number completely. From Heliopolis however, as you go up, Egypt is narrow; for on the one side a mountain-range belonging to Arabia stretches along by the side of it, going in a direction from the North towards the midday and the South Wind, tending upwards without a break to that which is called the Erythraian Sea, in which range are the stone- quarries which were used in cutting stone for the pyramids at Memphis. On this side then the mountain ends where I have said, and then takes a turn back; and where it is widest, as I was informed, it is a journey of two months across from East to West; and the borders of it which turn towards the East are said to produce frankincense. Such then is the nature of this mountain-range; and on the side of Egypt towards Libya another range extends, rocky and enveloped in sand: in this are the pyramids, and it runs in the same direction as those parts of the Arabian mountains which go towards the midday. So then, I say, from Heliopolis the land has no longer a great extent so far as it belongs to Egypt, and for about four days' sail up the river Egypt properly so called is ˙narrow: and the space between the mountain- ranges which have been mentioned is plain-land, but where it is narrowest it did not seem to me to exceed two hundred furlongs from the Arabian mountains to those which are called the Libyan. After this again Egypt is broad. Such is the nature of this land: and from Heliopolis to Thebes is a voyage up the river of nine days, and the distance of the journey in furlongs is four thousand eight hundred and sixty, the number of *schoines* being eighty-one. If these measures of Egypt in furlongs be put together, the result is as follows:--I have already before this shown that the distance along the sea amounts to three thousand six hundred furlongs, and I will now declare what the distance is inland from the sea to Thebes, namely six thousand one hundred and twenty furlongs: and again the distance from Thebes to the city called Elephantine is one thousand eight hundred furlongs.

Of this land then, concerning which I have spoken, it seemed to myself also, according as the priests said, that the greater part had been won as an addition by the Egyptians; for it was evident to me that the space between the aforesaid mountain-ranges, which lie above the city of Memphis, once was a gulf of the sea, like the regions about Ilion and Teuthrania and Ephesos and the plain of the Maiander, if it be permitted to compare small things with great; and small these are in comparison, for of the rivers which heaped up the soil in those regions none is worthy to be compared in volume with a single one of the mouths of the Nile, which has five mouths. Moreover there are other rivers also, not in size at all equal to the Nile, which have performed great feats; of which I can mention the names of several, and especially the Acheloos, which flowing through Acarnania and so issuing out into the sea has already made half of the Echinades from islands into mainland. Now there is in the land of Arabia, not far from Egypt, a gulf of the sea running in from that which is called the Erythraian Sea, very long and narrow, as I am about to tell. With respect to the length of the voyage along it, one who set out from the innermost point to sail out through it into the open sea, would spend forty days upon the voyage, using oars; and with respect to breadth, where the gulf is broadest it is half a day's sail across: and there is in it an ebb and flow of tide every day. Just such another gulf I suppose that Egypt was, and that the one ran in towards Ethiopia from the Northern Sea, and the other, the Arabian, of which I am about to speak, tended from the South towards Syria, the gulfs boring in so as almost to meet at their extreme points, and passing by one another with but a small space left between. If then the stream of the Nile should turn aside into this Arabian gulf, what would hinder that gulf from being filled up with silt as the river continued to flow, at all events within a period of twenty thousand years? Indeed, for my part, I am of the opinion that it would be filled up even within ten thousand years. How, then, in all the time that has elapsed before I came into being should not a gulf be filled up even of much greater size than this by a river so great and so active? As regards Egypt then, I both believe those who say that things are so, and for myself also I am strongly of opinion that they are so; because I have observed that Egypt runs out into the sea further than the adjoining land, and that shells are found upon the mountains of it, and an efflorescence of salt forms upon the surface, so that even the pyramids are being eaten away by it, and moreover that of all the mountains of Egypt, the range which lies above Memphis is the only one which has sand: besides which I notice that Egypt resembles neither the land of Arabia, which borders upon it, nor Libya, nor yet Syria (for they are Syrians who dwell in the parts of Arabia lying along the sea), but that it has soil which is black and easily breaks up, seeing that it is in truth mud and silt brought down from Ethiopia by the river: but the soil of Libya, we know, is reddish in colour and rather sandy, while that of Arabia and Syria is somewhat clayey and rocky. The priests also gave me a strong proof concerning this land as follows, namely that in the reign of king Moiris, whenever the river reached a height of at least eight cubits it watered Egypt below Memphis; and not yet nine hundred years had gone by since the death of Moiris, when I heard these things from the priests: now however, unless the river rises to sixteen cubits, or fifteen at the least, it does not go over the land. I think too that those Egyptians who dwell below the lake of Moiris and especially in that region which is called the Delta, if that land continues to grow in height according to this proportion and to increase similarly in extent, will suffer for all remaining time, from the Nile not overflowing their land, that same thing which they themselves said that the Hellenes would at some time suffer: for hearing that the whole land of the Hellenes has rain and is not watered by rivers as theirs is, they said that the Hellenes would at some time be disappointed of a great hope and would suffer the ills of famine. This saying means that if the god shall not send them rain, but shall allow drought to prevail for a long time, the Hellenes will be destroyed by hunger; for they have in fact no other supply of water to save them except from Zeus alone. This has been rightly said by the Egyptians with reference to the Hellenes: but now let me tell how matters are with the Egyptians themselves in their turn. If, in accordance with what I before said, their land below Memphis (for this is that which is increasing) shall continue to increase in height according to the same proportion as in the past time, assuredly those Egyptians who dwell here will suffer famine, if their land shall not have rain nor the river be able to go over their fields. It is certain however that now they gather in fruit from the earth with less labour than any other men and also with less than the other Egyptians; for they have no labour in breaking up furrows with a plough nor in hoeing nor in any other of those labours which other men have about a crop; but when the river has come up of itself and watered their fields and after watering has left them again, then each man sows his own field and turns into it swine, and when he has trodden the seed into the ground by means of the swine, after that he waits for the harvest, and when he has threshed the corn by means of the swine, then he gathers it in.

If we desire to follow the opinions of the Ionians as regards Egypt, who say that the Delta alone is Egypt, reckoning its sea-coast to be from the watch-tower called of Perseus to the fish-curing houses of Pelusion, a distance of forty schoines, and counting it to extend inland as far as the city of Kercasoros, where the Nile divides and runs to Pelusion and Canobos, while as for the rest of Egypt, they assign it partly to Libya and partly to Arabia,--if, I say, we should follow this account, we should thereby declare that in former times the Egyptians had no land to live in; for, as we have seen, their Delta at any rate is alluvial, and has appeared (so to speak) lately, as the Egyptians themselves say and as my opinion is. If then at the first there was no land for them to live in, why did they waste their labour to prove that they had come into being before all other men? They needed not to have made trial of the children to see what language they would first utter. However I am not

11

of the opinion that the Egyptians came into being at the same time as that which is called by the Ionians the Delta, but that they existed always ever since the human race came into being, and that as their land advanced forwards, many of them were left in their first abodes and many came down gradually to the lower parts. At least it is certain that in old times Thebes had the name of Egypt, and of this the circumference measures six thousand one hundred and twenty furlongs.

If then we judge aright of these matters, the opinion of the Ionians about Egypt is not sound: but if the judgment of the Ionians is right, I declare that neither the Hellenes nor the Ionians themselves know how to reckon since they say that the whole earth is made up of three divisions, Europe, Asia, and Libya: for they ought to count in addition to these the Delta of Egypt, since it belongs neither to Asia nor to Libya; for at least it cannot be the river Nile by this reckoning which divides Asia from Libya, but the Nile is cleft at the point of this Delta so as to flow round it, and the result is that this land would come between Asia and Libya.

We dismiss then our opinion of the Ionians, and express a judgment of our own on this matter also, that Egypt is all that land which is inhabited by Egyptians, just as Kilikia is that which is inhabited by Kilikians and Assyria that which is inhabited by Assyrians, and we know of no boundary properly speaking between Asia and Libya except the borders of Egypt. If however we shall adopt the opinion which is commonly held by the Hellenes, we shall suppose that the whole of Egypt, beginning from the Cataract and the city of Elephantine, is divided into two parts and that it thus partakes of both the names, since one side will thus belong to Libya and the other to Asia; for the Nile from the Cataract onwards flows to the sea cutting Egypt through in the midst; and as far as the city of Kercasoros the Nile flows in one single stream, but from this city onwards it is parted into three ways; and one, which is called the Pelusian mouth, turns towards the East; the second of the ways goes towards the West, and this is called the Canobic mouth; but that one of the ways which is straight runs thus,--when the river in its course downwards comes to the point of the Delta, then it cuts the Delta through the midst and so issues out to the sea. In this we have a portion of the water of the river which is not the smallest nor the least famous, and it is called the Sebennytic mouth. There are also two other mouths which part off from the Sebennytic and go to the sea, and these are called, one the Saitic, the other the Mendesian mouth. The Bolbitinitic, and Bucolic mouths, on the other hand, are not natural but made by digging. Moreover, also the answer given by the Oracle of Ammon bears witness in support of my opinion that Egypt is of the extent which I declare it to be in my account; and of this answer I heard after I had formed my own opinion about Egypt. For those of the city of Marea and of Apis, dwelling in the parts of Egypt which border on Libya, being of opinion themselves that they were Libyans and not Egyptians, and also being burdened by the rules of religious service, because they desired not to be debarred from the use of cows' flesh, sent to Ammon saying that they had nought in common with the Egyptians, for they dwelt outside the Delta and agreed with them in nothing; and they said they desired that it might be lawful for them to eat everything without distinction. The god however did not permit them to do so, but said that that land was Egypt where the Nile came over and watered, and that those were Egyptians who dwelling below the city of Elephantine drank of that river. Thus was it answered to them by the Oracle about this: and the Nile, when it is in flood, goes over not only the Delta but also of the land which is called Libyan and of that which is called Arabian sometimes as much as two days' journey on each side, and at times even more than this or at times less.

As regards the nature of the river, neither from the priests nor yet from any other man was I able to obtain any knowledge: and I was desirous especially to learn from them about these matters, namely why the Nile comes down increasing in volume from the summer solstice onwards for a hundred days, and then, when it has reached the number of these days, turns and goes back, failing in its stream, so that through the whole winter season it continues to be low, and until the summer solstice returns. Of none of these things was I able to receive any account from the Egyptians, when I inquired of them what power the Nile has whereby it is of a nature opposite to that of all other rivers. And I made inquiry, desiring to know both this which I say and also why, unlike all other rivers, it does not give rise to any breezes blowing from it. However some of the Hellenes who desired to gain distinction for cleverness have given an account of this water in three different ways: two of these I do not think it worth while even to speak of except only to indicate their nature; of which the one says that the Etesian Winds are the cause that makes the river rise, by preventing the Nile from flowing out into the sea. But often the Etesian Winds fail and yet the Nile does the same work as it is wont to do; and moreover, if these were the cause, all the other rivers also which flow in a direction opposed to the Etesian Winds ought to have been affected in the same way as the Nile, and even more, in as much as they are smaller and present to them a feebler flow of streams: but there are many of these rivers in Syria and many also in Libya, and they are affected in no such manner as the Nile. The second way shows more ignorance than that which has been mentioned, and it is more marvellous to tell; for it says that the river produces these effects because it flows from the Ocean, and that the Ocean flows round the whole earth. The third of the ways is much the most specious, but nevertheless it is the most mistaken of all: for indeed this way has no more truth in it than the rest, alleging as it does that the Nile flows from melting snow; whereas it flows out of Libya through the midst of the Ethiopians, and so comes out into Egypt. How then should it flow from snow, when it flows from the hottest parts to those which are cooler? And indeed most of the facts are such as to convince a man (one at least who is capable of reasoning about such matters), that it is not at all likely that it flows from snow. The first and greatest evidence is afforded by the winds, which blow hot from these regions; the second is that the land is rainless always and without frost, whereas after snow has fallen rain must necessarily come within five days, so that if it snowed in those parts rain would fall there; the third evidence is afforded by the people dwelling there, who are of a black colour by reason of the burning heat. Moreover kites and swallows remain there through the year and do not leave the land; and cranes flying from the cold weather which comes on in the region of Scythia come regularly to these parts for wintering: if then it snowed ever so little in that land through which the Nile flows and in which it has its rise, none of these things would take place, as necessity compels us to admit. As for him who talked about the Ocean, he carried his tale into the region of the unknown, and so he need not be refuted; since I for my part know of no river Ocean existing, but I think that Homer or one of the poets who were before him invented the name and introduced it into his verse.

If, however after I have found fault with the opinions proposed, I am bound to declare an opinion of my own about the matters which are in doubt, I will tell what to my mind is the reason why the Nile increases in the summer. In the winter season the Sun, being driven away from his former path through the heaven by the stormy winds, comes to the upper parts of Libya. If one would set forth the matter in the shortest way, all has now been said; for whatever region this god approaches most and stands directly above, this it may reasonably be supposed is most in want of water, and its native streams of rivers are dried up most. However, to set it forth at greater length, thus it is:--the Sun passing in his course by the upper parts of Libya, does thus, that is to say, since at all times the air in those parts is clear and the country is warm, because there are no cold winds, in passing through it the Sun does just as he was wont to do in the summer, when going through the midst of the heaven, that is he draws to himself the water, and having drawn it he drives it away to the upper parts of the country, and the winds take it up and scattering it abroad melt it into rain; so it is natural that the winds which blow from this region, namely the South and South-west Winds, should be much the most rainy of all the winds. I think however that the Sun does not send away from himself all the water of the Nile of each year, but that also he lets some remain behind with himself. Then when the winter becomes milder, the Sun returns back again to the midst of the heaven, and from that time onwards he draws equally from all rivers; but in the meantime they flow in large volume, since water of rain mingles with them in great quantity, because their country receives rain then and is filled with torrent streams. In summer however they are weak, since not only the showers of rain fail them, but also they are drawn by the Sun. The Nile however, alone of all rivers, not having rain and being drawn by the Sun, naturally

14

flows during this time of winter in much less than its proper volume, that is much less than in summer; for then it is drawn equally with all the other waters, but in winter it bears the burden alone. Thus I suppose the Sun to be the cause of these things. He also is the cause in my opinion that the air in these parts is dry, since he makes it so by scorching up his path through the heaven: thus summer prevails always in the upper parts of Libya.

If, however the station of the seasons had been changed, and where now in the heaven are placed the North Wind and winter, there was the station of the South Wind and of the midday, and where now is placed the South Wind, there was the North, if this had been so, the Sun being driven from the midst of the heaven by the winter and the North Wind would go to the upper parts of Europe, just as now he comes to the upper parts of Libya, and passing in his course throughout the whole of Europe I suppose he would do to the Ister that which he now works upon the Nile. As to the breeze, why none blows from the river, my opinion is that from very hot places it is not natural that anything should blow, and that a breeze is wont to blow from something cold.

Let these matters then be as they are and as they were at the first: but as to the sources of the Nile, not one either of the Egyptians or of the Libyans or of the Hellenes, who came to speech with me, professed to know anything, except the scribe of the sacred treasury of Athene at the city of Sais in Egypt. To me however this man seemed not to be speaking seriously when he said that he had certain knowledge of it; and he said as follows, namely that there were two mountains of which the tops ran up to a sharp point, situated between the city of Syene, which is in the district of Thebes, and Elephantine, and the names of the mountains were, of the one Crophi and of the other Mophi. From the middle between these mountains flowed (he said) the sources of the Nile, which were fathomless in depth, and half of the water flowed to Egypt and towards the North Wind, the other half to Ethiopia and the South Wind. As for the fathomless depth of the source, he said that Psammetichos king of Egypt came to a trial of this matter; for he had a rope twisted of many thousand fathoms and let it down in this place, and it found no bottom. By this the scribe (if this which he told was really as he said) gave me to understand that there were certain strong eddies there and a backward flow, and that since the water dashed against the mountains, therefore the sounding-line could not come to any bottom when it was let down. From no other person was I able to learn anything about this matter; but for the rest I learnt so much as here follows by the most diligent inquiry; for I went myself as an eye-witness as far as the city of Elephantine and from that point onwards I gathered knowledge by report. From the city of Elephantine as one goes up the river there is country which slopes steeply; so that here one must attach ropes to the vessel on both sides, as one fastens an ox, and so make one's way onward; and if the rope break, the vessel is gone at once, carried away by the violence of the stream. Through this country it is a voyage of about four days in length, and in this part the Nile is winding like the river Maiander, and the distance amounts to twelve *schoines*, which one must traverse in this manner. Then you will come to a level plain, in which the Nile flows round an island named Tachompso. (Now in the regions above the Elephantine there dwell Ethiopians at once succeeding, who also occupy half of the island, and Egyptians the other half.) Adjoining this island there is a great lake, round which dwell Ethiopian nomad tribes; and when you have sailed through this you will come to the stream of the Nile again, which flows into this lake. After this you will disembark and make a journey by land of forty days; for in the Nile sharp rocks stand forth out of the water, and there are many reefs, by which it is not possible for a vessel to pass. Then after having passed through this country in the forty days which I have said, you will embark again in another vessel and sail for twelve days; and after this you will come to a great city called Meroe. This city is said to be the mother-city of all the other Ethiopians: and they who dwell in it reverence of the gods Zeus and Dionysos alone, and these they greatly honour; and they have an Oracle of Zeus established, and make warlike marches whensoever the god commands them by prophesyings and to whatsoever place he commands. Sailing from this city you will come to the "Deserters" in another period of time equal to that in which you came from Elephantine to the mother-city of the Ethiopians. Now the name of these "Deserters" is *Asmach*, and this word signifies, when translated into the tongue of the Hellenes, "those who stand on the left hand of the king." These were two hundred and forty thousand Egyptians of the warrior class, who revolted and went over to these Ethiopians for the following cause:--In the reign of Psammetichos garrisons were set, one towards the Ethiopians at the city of Elephantine, another towards the Arabians and Assyrians at Daphnai of Pelusion, and another towards Libya at Marea: and even in my own time the garrisons of the Persians too are ordered in the same manner as these were in the reign of Psammetichos, for both at Elephantine and at Daphnai the Persians have outposts. The Egyptians then of whom I speak had served as outposts for three years and no one relieved them from their guard; accordingly they took counsel together, and adopting a common plan they all in a body revolted from Psammetichos and set out for Ethiopia. Hearing this Psammetichos set forth in pursuit, and when he came up with them he entreated them much and endeavoured to persuade them not to desert the gods of their country and their children and wives: upon which it is said that one of them pointed to his privy member and said that wherever this was, there would they have both children and wives. When these came to Ethiopia they gave themselves over to the king of the Ethiopians; and he rewarded them as follows:--there were certain of the Ethiopians who had come to be at variance with him; and he bade them drive these out and dwell in their land. So since these men settled in the land of the

16

Ethiopians, the Ethiopians have come to be of milder manners, from having learnt the customs of the Egyptians.

The Nile then, besides the part of its course which is in Egypt, is known as far as a four months' journey by river and land: for that is the number of months which are found by reckoning to be spent in going from Elephantine to these "Deserters": and the river runs from the West and the setting of the sun. But what comes after that point no one can clearly say; for this land is desert by reason of the burning heat. This much however I heard from men of Kyrene, who told me that they had been to the Oracle of Ammon, and had come to speech with Etearchos king of the Ammonians: and it happened that after speaking of other matters they fell to discourse about the Nile and how no one knew the sources of it; and Etearchos said that once there came to him men of the Nasamonians (this is a Libyan race which dwells in the Syrtis, and also in the land to the East of the Syrtis reaching to no great distance), and when the Nasamonians came and were asked by him whether they were able to tell him anything more than he knew about the desert parts of Libya, they said that there had been among them certain sons of chief men, who were of unruly disposition; and these when they grew up to be men had devised various other extravagant things and also they had told off by lot five of themselves to go to see the desert parts of Libya and to try whether they could discover more than those who had previously explored furthest: for in those parts of Libya which are by the Northern Sea, beginning from Egypt and going as far as the headland of Soloeis, which is the extreme point of Libya, Libyans (and of them many races) extend along the whole coast, except so much as the Hellenes and Phenicians hold; but in the upper parts, which lie above the sea-coast and above those people whose land comes down to the sea, Libya is full of wild beasts; and in the parts above the land of wild beasts it is full of sand, terribly waterless and utterly desert. These young men then (said they), being sent out by their companions well furnished with supplies of water and provisions, went first through the inhabited country, and after they had passed through this they came to the country of wild beasts, and after this they passed through the desert, making their journey towards the West Wind; and having passed through a great tract of sand in many days, they saw at last trees growing in a level place; and having come up to them, they were beginning to pluck the fruit which was upon the trees: but as they began to pluck it, there came upon them small men, of less stature than men of the common size, and these seized them and carried them away; and neither could the Nasamonians understand anything of their speech nor could those who were carrying them off understand anything of the speech of the Nasamonians; and they led them (so it was said) through very great swamps, and after passing through these they came to a city in which all the men were in size like those who carried them off and in colour of skin black; and by the city ran a great river, which ran from the West towards the sunrising, and in it were seen crocodiles. Of the account given by Etearchos the Ammonian let so much suffice as is here said, except that, as the men of Kyrene told me, he alleged that the Nasamonians returned safe home, and that the people to whom they had come were all wizards. Now this river which ran by the city, Etearchos conjectured to be the Nile, and moreover reason compels us to think so; for the Nile flows from Libya and cuts Libya through in the midst, and as I conjecture, judging of what is not known by that which is evident to the view, it starts at a distance from its mouth equal to that of the Ister: for the river Ister begins from the Keltoi and the city of Pyrene and so runs that it divides Europe in the midst (now the Keltoi are outside the Pillars of Heracles and border upon the Kynesians, who dwell furthest towards the sunset of all those who have their dwelling in Europe): and the Ister ends, having its course through the whole of Europe, by flowing into the Euxine Sea at the place where the Milesians have their settlement of Istria. Now the Ister, since it flows through land which is inhabited, is known by the reports of many; but of the sources of the Nile no one can give an account, for the part of Libya through which it flows is uninhabited and desert. About its course however so much as it was possible to learn by the most diligent inquiry has been told; and it runs out into Egypt. Now Egypt lies nearly opposite to the mountain districts of Kilikia; and from thence to Sinope, which lies upon the Euxine Sea, is a journey in the same straight line of five days for a man without encumbrance; and Sinope lies opposite to the place where the Ister runs out into the sea: thus I think that the Nile passes through the whole of Libya and is of equal measure with the Ister.

CHAPTER 2

Of the Nile then let so much suffice as has been said. Of Egypt however I shall make my report at length, because it has wonders more in number than any other land, and works too it has to show as much as any land, which are beyond expression great: for this reason then more shall be said concerning it.

The Egyptians in agreement with their climate, which is unlike any other, and with the river, which shows a nature different from all other rivers, established for themselves manners and customs in a way opposite to other men in almost all matters: for among them the women frequent the market and carry on trade, while the men remain at home and weave; and whereas others weave pushing the woof upwards, the Egyptians push it downwards: the men carry their burdens upon their heads and the women upon their shoulders: the women make water standing up and the men crouching down: they ease themselves in their houses and they eat without in the streets, alleging as reason for this that it is right to do secretly the things that are unseemly though necessary, but those which are not unseemly, in public: no woman is a minister either of male or female divinity, but men of all, both male and female: to support their parents the sons are in no way compelled, if they do not desire to do so, but the daughters are forced to do so, be they never so unwilling. The priests of the gods in other lands wear long hair, but in Egypt they shave their heads: among other men the custom is that in mourning those whom the matter concerns most nearly have their hair cut short, but the Egyptians, when deaths occur, let their hair grow long, both that on the head and that on the chin, having before been close shaven: other men have their daily living separated from beasts, but the Egyptians have theirs together with beasts: other men live on wheat and on barley, but to any one of the Egyptians who makes his living on these it is a great reproach; they make their bread of maize, which some call spelt: they knead dough with their feet and clay with their hands, with which also they gather up dung: and whereas other men, except such as have learnt otherwise from the Egyptians, have their members as nature made them, the Egyptians practice circumcision: as to garments, the men wear two each and the women but one: and whereas others make fast the rings and ropes of the sails outside the ship, the Egyptians do this inside: finally in the writing of characters and reckoning with pebbles, while the Hellenes carry the hand from the left to the right, the Egyptians do this from the right to the left; and doing so they say that they do it themselves rightwise and the Hellenes leftwise: and they use two kinds of characters for writing, of which the one kind is called sacred and the other common.

They are religious excessively beyond all other men, and with regard to this they have customs as follows:--they drink from cups of bronze and rinse them out every day, and not some only do this but all: they wear garments of linen always newly washed, and this they make a special point of practice: they circumcise themselves for the sake of cleanliness, preferring to be clean rather than comely. The priests shave themselves all over their body every other day, so that no lice or any other foul thing may come to be upon them when they minister to the gods; and the priests wear garments of linen only and sandals of papyrus, and any other garment they may not take nor other sandals; these wash themselves in cold water twice in a day and twice again in the night; and other religious services they perform (one may almost say) of infinite number. They enjoy also good things not a few, for they do not consume or spend anything of their own substance, but there is sacred bread baked for them and they have each great quantity of flesh of oxen and geese coming in to them each day, and also wine of grapes is given to them; but it is not permitted to them to taste of fish: beans moreover the Egyptians do not at all sow in their land, and those which they grow they neither eat raw nor boil for food; nay the priests do not endure even to look upon them, thinking this to be an unclean kind of pulse: and there is not one priest only for each of the gods but many, and of them one is chief-priest, and whenever a priest dies his son is appointed to his place.

The males of the ox kind they consider to belong to Epaphos, and on account of him they test them in the following manner:--If the priest sees one single black hair upon the beast he counts it not clean for sacrifice; and one of the priests who is appointed for the purpose makes investigation of these matters, both when the beast is standing upright and when it is lying on its back, drawing out its tongue moreover, to see if it is clean in respect of the appointed signs, which I shall tell of in another part of the history: he looks also at the hairs of the tail to see if it has them growing in a natural manner; and if it be clean in respect of all these things, he marks it with a piece of papyrus, rolling this round the horns, and then when he has plastered sealing-earth over it he sets upon it the seal of his signet-ring, and after that they take the animal away. But for one who sacrifices a beast not sealed the penalty appointed is death. In this way then the beast is tested; and their appointed manner of sacrifice is as follows:--they lead the sealed beast to the altar where they happen to be sacrificing, and then kindle a fire: after that, having poured libations of wine over the altar so that it runs down upon the victim and having called upon the god, they cut its throat, and having cut its throat they sever the head from the body. The body then of the beast they flay, but upon the head they make many imprecations first, and then they who have a market and Hellenes sojourning among them for trade, these carry it to the market-place and sell it, while they who have no Hellenes among them cast it away into the river: and this is the form of imprecations which they utter upon the heads, praying that if any evil be about to befall either themselves who are offering sacrifice or the land of Egypt in general, it may come rather upon this head. Now as regards the heads of the beasts which are sacrificed and the pouring over them of the wine, all the Egyptians have the same customs equally for all their sacrifices; and by reason of this custom none of the Egyptians eat of the head either of this or of any other kind of animal: but the manner of disembowelling the victims and of burning them is appointed among them differently for different sacrifices; I shall speak however of the sacrifices to that goddess whom they regard as the greatest of all, and to whom they celebrate the greatest feast.--When they have flayed the bullock and made imprecation, they take out the whole of its lower entrails but leave in the body the upper entrails and the fat; and they sever from it the legs and the end of the loin and the shoulders and the neck: and this done, they fill the rest of the body of the animal with consecrated loaves and honey and raisins and figs and frankincense and myrrh and every other kind of spices, and having filled it with these they offer it, pouring over it great abundance of oil. They make their sacrifice after fasting, and while the offerings are being burnt, they all beat themselves for mourning, and when they have finished beating themselves they set forth as a feast that which they left unburnt of the sacrifice. The clean males then of the ox kind, both full-grown animals and calves, are sacrificed by all the Egyptians; the females however they may not sacrifice, but these are sacred to Isis; for the figure of Isis is in the form of a woman with cow's horns, just as the Hellenes present Io in pictures, and all the Egyptians without distinction reverence cows far more than any other kind of cattle; for which reason neither man nor woman of the Egyptian race would kiss a man who is a Hellene on the mouth, nor will they use a knife or roasting-spits or a caldron belonging to a Hellene, nor taste the flesh even of a clean animal if it has been cut with the knife of a Hellene. And the cattle of this kind which die they bury in the following manner:--the females they cast into the river, but the males they bury, each people in the suburb of their town, with one of the horns, or sometimes both, protruding to mark the place; and when the bodies have rotted away and the appointed time comes on, then to each city comes a boat from that which is called the island of Prosopitis (this is in the Delta, and the extent of its circuit is nine *schoines*). In this island of Prosopitis is situated, besides many other cities, that one from which the boats come to take up the bones of the oxen, and the name of the city is Atarbechis, and in it there is set up a holy temple of Aphrodite. From this city many go abroad in various directions, some to one city and others to another, and when they have dug up the bones of the oxen they carry them off, and coming together they bury them in one single place. In the same manner as they bury the oxen they bury also their other cattle when they die; for about them also they have the same law laid down, and these also they abstain from killing.

Now all who have a temple set up to the Theban Zeus or who are of the district of Thebes, these, I say, all sacrifice goats and abstain from sheep: for not all the Egyptians equally reverence the same gods, except only Isis and Osiris (who they say is Dionysos), these they all reverence alike: but they who have a temple of Mendes or belong to the Mendesian district, these abstain from goats and sacrifice sheep. Now the men of Thebes and those who after their example abstain from sheep, say that this custom was established among them for the cause which follows:--Heracles (they say) had an earnest desire to see Zeus, and Zeus did not desire to be seen of him; and at last when Heracles was urgent in entreaty Zeus contrived this device, that is to say, he flayed a ram and held in front of him the head of the ram which he had cut off, and he put on over him the fleece and then showed himself to him. Hence the Egyptians make the image of Zeus with the face of a ram; and the Ammonians do so also after their example, being settlers both from the Egyptians and from the Ethiopians, and using a language which is a medley of both tongues: and in my opinion it is from this god that the Egyptians call Zeus *Amun*. The Thebans then do not sacrifice rams but hold them sacred for this reason; on one day however in the year, on the feast of Zeus, they cut up in the same manner and flay one single ram and cover with its skin the image of Zeus, and then they bring up to it another image of Heracles. This done, all who are in the temple beat themselves in lamentation for the ram, and then they bury it in a sacred tomb.

About Heracles I heard the account given that he was of the number of the twelve gods; but of the other Heracles whom the Hellenes know I was not able to hear in any part of Egypt: and moreover to prove that the Egyptians did not take the name of Heracles from the Hellenes, but rather the Hellenes from the Egyptians,--that is to say those of the Hellenes who gave the name Heracles to the son of Amphitryon,-- of that, I say, besides many other evidences there is chiefly this, namely that the parents of this Heracles, Amphitryon and Alcmene, were both of Egypt by descent, and also that the Egyptians say that they do not know the names either of Poseidon or of the Dioscuroi, nor have these been accepted by them as gods among the other gods; whereas if they had received from the Hellenes the name of any divinity, they would naturally have preserved the memory of these most of all, assuming that in those times as now some of the Hellenes were wont to make voyages and were seafaring folk, as I suppose and as my judgment compels me to think; so that the Egyptians would have learnt the names of these gods even more than that of Heracles. In fact however Heracles is a very ancient Egyptian god; and (as they say themselves) it is seventeen thousand years to the beginning of the reign of Amasis from the time when the twelve gods, of whom they count that Heracles is one, were begotten of the eight gods. I moreover, desiring to know something certain of these matters so far as might be, made a voyage also to Tyre of Phenicia, hearing that in that place there was a holy temple of Heracles; and I saw that it was richly furnished with many votive offerings besides, and especially there were in it two pillars, the one of pure gold and the other of an emerald stone of such size as to shine by night: and having come to speech with the priests of the god, I asked them how long a time it was since their temple had been set up: and these also I found to be at variance with the Hellenes, for they said that at the same time when Tyre was founded, the temple of the god also had been set up, and that it was a period of two thousand three hundred years since their people began to dwell at Tyre. I saw also at Tyre another temple of Heracles, with the surname Thasian; and I came to Thasos also and there I found a temple of Heracles set up by the Phenicians, who had sailed out to seek for Europa and had colonised Thasos; and these things happened full five generations of men before Heracles the son of Amphitryon was born in Hellas. So then my inquiries show clearly that Heracles is an ancient god, and those of the Hellenes seem to me to act most rightly who have two temples of Heracles set up, and who sacrifice to the one as an immortal god and with the title Olympian, and make offerings of the dead to the other as a hero. Moreover, besides many other stories which the Hellenes tell without due consideration, this tale is especially foolish which they tell about Heracles, namely that when he came to Egypt, the Egyptians put on him wreaths and led him forth in procession to sacrifice him to Zeus; and he for some time kept quiet, but when they were beginning the sacrifice of him at the altar, he betook himself to prowess and slew them all. I for my part am of opinion that the Hellenes when they tell this tale are altogether without knowledge of the nature and customs of the Egyptians; for how should they for whom it is not lawful to sacrifice even beasts, except swine and the males of oxen and calves (such of them as are clean) and geese, how should these sacrifice human beings? Besides this, how is it in nature possible that Heracles, being one person only and moreover a man (as they assert), should slay many myriads? Having said so much of these matters, we pray that we may have grace from both the gods and the heroes for our speech.

Now the reason why those of the Egyptians whom I have mentioned do not sacrifice goats, female or male, is this:--the Mendesians count Pan to be one of the eight gods (now these eight gods they say came into being before the twelve gods), and the painters and image-makers represent in painting and in sculpture the figure of Pan, just as the Hellenes do, with goat's face and legs, not supposing him to be really like this but to resemble the other gods; the cause however why they represent him in this form I prefer not to say. The Mendesians then reverence all goats and the males more than the females (and the goatherds too have greater honour than other herdsmen), but of the goats one especially is reverenced, and when he dies there is great mourning in all the Mendesian district: and both the goat and Pan are called in the Egyptian tongue *Mendes*. Moreover in my lifetime there happened in that district this marvel, that is to say a he-goat had intercourse with a woman publicly, and this was so done that all men might have evidence of it.

The pig is accounted by the Egyptians an abominable animal; and first, if any of them in passing by touch a pig, he goes into the river and dips himself forthwith in the water together with his garments; and then too swineherds, though they may be native Egyptians, unlike all others, do not enter any of the temples in Egypt, nor is anyone willing to give his daughter in marriage to one of them or to take a wife from among them; but the swineherds both give in marriage to one another and take from one another. Now to the other gods the Egyptians do not think it right to sacrifice swine; but to the Moon and to Dionysos alone at the same time and on the same full-moon they sacrifice swine, and then eat their flesh: and as to the reason why, when they abominate swine at all their other feasts, they sacrifice them at this, there is a story told by the Egyptians; and this story I know, but it is not a seemly one for me to tell. Now the sacrifice of the swine to the Moon is performed as follows:--when the priest has slain the victim, he puts together the end of the tail and the spleen and the caul, and covers them up with the whole of the fat of the animal which is about the paunch, and then he offers them with fire; and the rest of the flesh they eat on that day of full moon upon which they have held sacrifice, but on any day after this they will not taste of it: the poor however among them by reason of the scantiness of their means shape pigs of dough and having baked them they offer these as a sacrifice. Then for Dionysos on the eve of the festival each one kills a pig by cutting its throat before his own doors, and after that he gives the pig to the swineherd who sold it to him, to carry away again; and the rest of the feast of Dionysos is celebrated by the Egyptians in the same way as by the Hellenes in almost all things except choral dances, but instead of the *phallos* they have invented another contrivance, namely figures of about a cubit in height worked by strings, which women carry about the villages, with the privy member made to move and not much less in size than the rest of the body: and a flute goes before and they follow singing the praises of Dionysos. As to the reason why the figure has this member larger than is natural and moves it, though it moves no other part of the body, about this there is a sacred story told. Now I think that Melampus the son of Amytheon was not without knowledge of these rites of sacrifice, but was acquainted with them: for Melampus is he who first set forth to the Hellenes the name of Dionysos and the manner of sacrifice and the procession of the *phallos*. Strictly speaking indeed, he when he made it known did not take in the whole, but those wise men who came after him made it known more at large. Melampus then is he who taught of the *phallos* which is carried in procession for Dionysos, and from him the Hellenes learnt to do that which they do. I say then that Melampus being a man of ability contrived for himself

24

Zeus under a real oak-tree; as indeed it was natural that being an attendant of the sanctuary of Zeus at Thebes, she should there, in the place to which she had come, have a memory of him; and after this, when she got understanding of the Hellenic tongue, she established an Oracle, and she reported, I suppose, that her sister had been sold in Libya by the same Phenicians by whom she herself had been sold. Moreover, I think that the women were called doves by the people of Dodona for the reason that they were barbarians and because it seemed to them that they uttered voice like birds; but after a time (they say) the dove spoke with human voice, that is when the woman began to speak so that they could understand; but so long as she spoke a Barbarian tongue she seemed to them to be uttering voice like a bird: for if it had been really a dove, how could it speak with human voice? And in saying that the dove was black, they indicate that the woman was Egyptian. The ways of delivering oracles too at Thebes in Egypt and at Dodona closely resemble each other, as it happens, and also the method of divination by victims has come from Egypt.

Moreover, it is true also that the Egyptians were the first of men who made solemn assemblies and processions and approaches to the temples, and from them the Hellenes have learnt them, and my evidence for this is that the Egyptian celebrations of these have been held from a very ancient time, whereas the Hellenic were introduced but lately. The Egyptians hold their solemn assemblies not once in the year but often, especially and with the greatest zeal and devotion at the city of Bubastis for Artemis, and next at Busiris for Isis; for in this last-named city there is a very great temple of Isis, and this city stands in the middle of the Delta of Egypt; now Isis is in the tongue of the Hellenes Demeter: thirdly, they have a solemn assembly at the city of Sais for Athene, fourthly at Heliopolis for the Sun (Helios), fifthly at the city of Buto in honour of Leto, and sixthly at the city of Papremis for Ares. Now, when they are coming to the city of Bubastis they do as follows:--they sail men and women together, and a great multitude of each sex in every boat; and some of the women have rattles and rattle with them, while some of the men play the flute during the whole time of the voyage, and the rest, both women and men, sing and clap their hands; and when as they sail they come opposite to any city on the way they bring the boat to land, and some of the women continue to do as I have said, others cry aloud and jeer at the women in that city, some dance, and some stand up and pull up their garments. This they do by every city along the river-bank; and when they come to Bubastis they hold festival celebrating great sacrifices, and more wine of grapes is consumed upon that festival than during the whole of the rest of the year. To this place (so say the natives) they come together year by year even to the number of seventy myriads of men and women, besides children. Thus it is done here; and how they celebrate the festival in honour of Isis at the city of Busiris has been told by me before: for, as I said, they beat themselves in mourning after the sacrifice, all of them

27

both men and women, very many myriads of people; but for whom they beat themselves it is not permitted to me by religion to say: and so many as there are of the Carians dwelling in Egypt do this even more than the Egyptians themselves, inasmuch as they cut their foreheads also with knives; and by this it is manifested that they are strangers and not Egyptians. At the times when they gather together at the city of Sais for their sacrifices, on a certain night they all kindle lamps many in number in the open air round about the houses; now the lamps are saucers full of salt and oil mixed, and the wick floats by itself on the surface, and this burns during the whole night; and to the festival is given the name *Lychnocaia* (the lighting of lamps). Moreover those of the Egyptians who have not come to this solemn assembly observe the night of the festival and themselves also light lamps all of them, and thus not in Sais alone are they lighted, but over all Egypt: and as to the reason why light and honour are allotted to this night, about this there is a sacred story told. To Heliopolis and Buto they go year by year and do sacrifice only: but at Papremis they do sacrifice and worship as elsewhere, and besides that, when the sun begins to go down while some few of the priests are occupied with the image of the god, the greater number of them stand in the entrance of the temple with wooden clubs, and other persons to the number of more than a thousand men with purpose to perform a vow, these also having all of them staves of wood, stand in a body opposite to those: and the image, which is in a small shrine of wood covered over with gold, they take out on the day before to another sacred building. The few then who have been left about the image, draw a wain with four wheels, which bears the shrine and the image that is within the shrine, and the other priests standing in the gateway try to prevent it from entering, and the men who are under a vow come to the assistance of the god and strike them, while the others defend themselves. Then there comes to be a hard fight with staves, and they break one another's heads, and I am of opinion that many even die of the wounds they receive; the Egyptians however told me that no one died. This solemn assembly the people of the place say that they established for the following reason:--the mother of Ares, they say, used to dwell in this temple, and Ares, having been brought up away from her, when he grew up came thither desiring to visit his mother, and the attendants of his mother's temple, not having seen him before, did not permit him to pass in, but kept him away; and he brought men to help him from another city and handled roughly the attendants of the temple, and entered to visit his mother. Hence, they say, this exchange of blows has become the custom in honour of Ares upon his festival.

The Egyptians were the first who made it a point of religion not to lie with women in temples, nor to enter into temples after going away from women without first bathing: for almost all other men except the Egyptians and the Hellenes lie with women in temples and enter into a temple after going away from women without bathing, since they hold that there is no difference in this respect between men and beasts: for they say that they see beasts and the various kinds of birds coupling together both in the temples and in the sacred enclosures of the gods; if then this were not pleasing to the god, the beasts would not do so.

Thus do these defend that which they do, which by me is disallowed: but the Egyptians are excessively careful in their observances, both in other matters which concern the sacred rites and also in those which follow:--Egypt, though it borders upon Libya, does not very much abound in wild animals, but such as they have are one and all accounted by them sacred, some of them living with men and others not. But if I should say for what reasons the sacred animals have been thus dedicated, I should fall into discourse of matters pertaining to the gods, of which I most desire not to speak; and what I have actually said touching slightly upon them, I said because I was constrained by necessity. About these animals there is a custom of this kind:-- persons have been appointed of the Egyptians, both men and women, to provide the food for each kind of beast separately, and their office goes down from father to son; and those who dwell in the various cities perform vows to them thus, that is, when they make a vow to the god to whom the animal belongs, they shave the head of their children either the whole or the half or the third part of it, and then set the hair in the balance against silver, and whatever it weighs, this the man gives to the person who provides for the animals, and she cuts up fish of equal value and gives it for food to the animals. Thus food for their support has been appointed and if any one kill any of these animals, the penalty, if he do it with his own will, is death, and if against his will, such penalty as the priests may appoint: but whosoever shall kill an ibis or a hawk, whether it be with his will or against his will, must die. Of the animals that live with men there are great numbers, and would be many more but for the accidents which befall the cats. For when the females have produced young they are no longer in the habit of going to the males, and these seeking to be united with them are not able. To this end then they contrive as follows,--they either take away by force or remove secretly the young from the females and kill them (but after killing they do not eat them), and the females being deprived of their young and desiring more, therefore come to the males, for it is a creature that is fond of its young. Moreover when a fire occurs, the cats seem to be divinely possessed; for while the Egyptians stand at intervals and look after the cats, not taking any care to extinguish the fire, the cats slipping through or leaping over the men, jump into the fire; and when this happens, great mourning comes upon the Egyptians. And in whatever houses a cat has died by a natural death, all those who dwell in this house shave their eyebrows only, but those in which a dog has died shave their whole body and also their head. The cats when they are dead are carried away to sacred buildings in the city of

Bubastis, where after being embalmed they are buried; but the dogs they bury each people in their own city in sacred tombs; and the ichneumons are buried just in the same way as the dogs. The shrewmice however and the hawks they carry away to the city of Buto, and the ibises to Hermopolis; the bears (which are not commonly seen) and the wolves, not much larger in size than foxes, they bury on the spot where they are found lying.

Of the crocodile the nature is as follows:--during the four most wintry months this creature eats nothing: she has four feet and is an animal belonging to the land and the water both; for she produces and hatches eggs on the land, and the most part of the day she remains upon dry land, but the whole of the night in the river, for the water in truth is warmer than the unclouded open air and the dew. Of all the mortal creatures of which we have knowledge this grows to the greatest bulk from the smallest beginning; for the eggs which she produces are not much larger than those of geese and the newly-hatched young one is in proportion to the egg, but as he grows he becomes as much as seventeen cubits long and sometimes yet larger. He has eyes like those of a pig and teeth large and tusky, in proportion to the size of his body; but unlike all other beasts he grows no tongue, neither does he move his lower jaw, but brings the upper jaw towards the lower, being in this too unlike all other beasts. He has moreover strong claws and a scaly hide upon his back which cannot be pierced; and he is blind in the water, but in the air he is of a very keen sight. Since he has his living in the water he keeps his mouth all full within of leeches; and whereas all other birds and beasts fly from him, the trochilus is a creature which is at peace with him, seeing that from her he receives benefit; for the crocodile having come out of the water to the land and then having opened his mouth (this he is wont to do generally towards the West Wind), the trochilus upon that enters into his mouth and swallows down the leeches, and he being benefited is pleased and does no harm to the trochilus. Now for some of the Egyptians the crocodiles are sacred animals, and for others not so, but they treat them on the contrary as enemies: those however who dwell about Thebes and about the lake of Moiris hold them to be most sacred, and each of these two peoples keeps one crocodile selected from the whole number, which has been trained to tameness, and they put hanging ornaments of molten stone and of gold into the ears of these and anklets round the front feet, and they give them food appointed and victims of sacrifices and treat them as well as possible while they live, and after they are dead they bury them in sacred tombs, embalming them: but those who dwell about the city of Elephantine even eat them, not holding them to be sacred. They are called not crocodiles but *champsai*, and the Ionians gave them the name of crocodile, comparing their form to that of the crocodiles (lizards) which appear in their them and of various kinds: I shall describe that which to me seems the most worthy of being told. A man puts the back of a pig upon a

30

hook as bait, and lets it go into the middle of the river, while he himself upon the bank of the river has a young live pig, which he beats; and the crocodile hearing its cries makes for the direction of the sound, and when he finds the pig's back he swallows it down: then they pull, and when he is drawn out to land, first of all the hunter forthwith plasters up his eyes with mud, and having done so he very easily gets the mastery of him, but if he does not do so he has much trouble.

The river-horse is sacred in the district of Papremis, but for the other Egyptians he is not sacred; and this is the appearance which he presents: he is four-footed, cloven-hoofed like an ox, flat-nosed, with a mane like a horse and showing teeth like tusks, with a tail and voice like a horse and in size as large as the largest ox; and his hide is so exceedingly thick that when it has been dried shafts of javelins are made of it. There are moreover otters in the river, which they consider to be sacred: and of fish also they esteem that which is called the *lepidotos* to be sacred, and also the eel; and these they say are sacred to the Nile: and of birds the fox-goose.

There is also another sacred bird called the phoenix which I did not myself see except in painting, for in truth he comes to them very rarely, at intervals, as the people of Heliopolis say, of five hundred years; and these say that he comes regularly when his father dies; and if he be like the painting he is of this size and nature, that is to say, some of his feathers are of gold colour and others red, and in outline and size he is as nearly as possible like an eagle. This bird they say (but I cannot believe the story) contrives as follows:-- setting forth from Arabia he conveys his father, they say, to the temple of the Sun (Helios) plastered up in myrrh, and buries him in the temple of the Sun; and he conveys him thus:--he forms first an egg of myrrh as large as he is able to carry, and then he makes trial of carrying it, and when he has made trial sufficiently, then he hollows out the egg and places his father within it and plasters over with other myrrh that part of the egg where he hollowed it out to put his father in, and when his father is laid in it, it proves (they say) to be of the same weight as it was; and after he has plastered it up, he conveys the whole to Egypt to the temple of the Sun. Thus they say that this bird does.

There are also about Thebes sacred serpents, not at all harmful to men, which are small in size and have two horns growing from the top of the head: these they bury when they die in the temple of Zeus, for to this god they say that they are sacred. There is a region moreover in Arabia, situated nearly over against the city of Buto, to which place I came to inquire about the winged serpents: and when I came thither I saw bones of serpents and spines in quantity so great that it is impossible to make report of the number, and there were heaps of spines, some heaps large and others less large and others smaller still than these, and these heaps were many in number. This region in which the spines are scattered upon the ground is of the nature of an entrance from a narrow mountain pass to a great plain, which plain adjoins the plain in Egypt; and the story goes that at the beginning of spring winged serpents from Arabia fly towards Egypt, and the birds called ibises meet them at the entrance to this country and do not suffer the serpents to go by but kill them. On account of this deed it is (say the Arabians) that the ibis has come to be greatly honoured by the Egyptians, and the Egyptians also agree that it is for this reason that they honour these birds. The outward form of the ibis is this:-- it is a deep black all over, and has legs like those of a crane and a very curved beak, and in size it is about equal to a rail: this is the appearance of the black kind which fight with the serpents, but of those which most crowd round men's feet (for there are two several kinds of ibises) the head is bare and also the whole of the throat, and it is white in feathering except the head and neck and the extremities of the wings and the rump (in all these parts of which I have spoken it is a deep black), while in legs and in the form of the head it resembles the other. As for the serpent its form is like that of the watersnake; and it has wings not feathered but most nearly resembling the wings of the bat. Let so much suffice as has been said now concerning sacred animals.

CHAPTER 3

Of the Egyptians themselves, those who dwell in the part of Egypt which is sown for crops practise memory more than any other men and are the most learned in history by far of all those of whom I have had experience: and their manner of life is as follows:--For three successive days in each month they purge, hunting after health with emetics and clysters, and they think that all the diseases which exist are produced in men by the food on which they live: for the Egyptians are from other causes also the most healthy of all men next after the Libyans (in my opinion on account of the seasons, because the seasons do not change, for by the changes of things generally, and especially of the seasons, diseases are most apt to be produced in men), and as to their diet, it is as follows:--they eat bread, making loaves of maize, which they call *kyllestis*, and they use habitually a wine made out of barley, for vines they have not in their land. Of their fish some they dry in the sun and then eat them without cooking, others they eat cured in brine. Of birds they eat quails and ducks and small birds without cooking, after first curing them; and everything else which they have belonging to the class of birds or fishes, except such as have been set apart by them as sacred, they eat roasted or boiled. In the entertainments of the rich among them, when they have finished eating, a man bears round a wooden figure of a dead body in a coffin, made as like the reality as may be both by painting and carving, and measuring about a cubit or two cubits each way; and this he shows to each of those who are drinking together, saying: "When thou lookest upon this, drink and be merry, for thou shalt be such as this when thou art dead." Thus they do at their carousals. The customs which they practise are derived from their fathers and they do not acquire others in addition; but besides other customary things among them which are worthy of mention, they have one song, that of Linos, the same who is sung of both in Phenicia and in Cyprus and elsewhere, having however a name different according to the various nations. This song agrees exactly with that which the Hellenes sing calling on the name of Linos, so that besides many other things about which I wonder among those matters which concern Egypt, I wonder especially about this, namely whence they got the song of Linos. It is evident however that they have sung this song from immemorial time, and in the Egyptian tongue Linos is called Maneros. The Egyptians told me that he was the only son of him who first became king of Egypt, and that he died before his time and was honoured with these lamentations by the Egyptians, and that this was their first and only song. In another respect the Egyptians are in agreement with some of the Hellenes, namely with the Lacedemonians, but not with the rest, that is to say, the younger of them when they meet the elder give way and move out of the path, and when their elders approach, they rise out of their seat. In this which follows however they are not in agreement with any of the Hellenes,--instead of addressing one another in the roads they do reverence, lowering their hand down to their knee. They wear tunics of linen about their legs with fringes, which they call *calasiris*; above these they have garments of white wool thrown over: woolen garments however are not taken into the temples, nor are they buried with them, for this is not permitted by religion. In these points they are in agreement with the observances called Orphic and Bacchic (which are really Egyptian), and also with those of the Pythagoreans, for one who takes part in these mysteries is also forbidden by religious rule to be buried in woolen garments; and about this there is a sacred story told.

Besides these things the Egyptians have found out also to what god each month and each day belongs, and what fortunes a man will meet with who is born on any particular day, and how he will die, and what kind of a man he will be: and these inventions were taken up by those of the Hellenes who occupied themselves about poesy. Portents too have been found out by them more than by all other men besides; for when a portent has happened, they observe and write down the event which comes of it, and if ever afterwards anything resembling this happens, they believe that the event which comes of it will be similar. Their divination is ordered thus:--the art is assigned not to any man but to certain of the gods, for there are in their land Oracles of Heracles, of Apollo, of Athene, of Artemis, or Ares, and of Zeus, and moreover that which they hold most in honour of all, namely the Oracle of Leto which is in the city of Buto. The manner of divination however is not established among them according to the same fashion everywhere, but is different in different places. The art of medicine among them is distributed thus:--each physician is a physician of one disease and of no more; and the whole country is full of physicians, for some profess themselves to be physicians of the eyes, others of the head, others of the teeth, others of the affections of the stomach, and others of the more obscure ailments.

Their fashions of mourning and of burial are these:--Whenever any household has lost a man who is of any regard amongst them, the whole number of women of that house forthwith plaster over their heads or even their faces with mud. Then leaving the corpse within the house they go themselves to and fro about the city and beat themselves, with their garments bound up by a girdle and their breasts exposed, and with them go all the women who are related to the dead man, and on the other side the men beat themselves, they too having their garments bound up by a girdle; and when they have done this, they then convey the body to the embalming. In this occupation certain persons employ themselves regularly and inherit this as a craft. These, whenever a corpse is conveyed to them, show to those who brought it wooden models of corpses made like reality by painting, and the best of

34

the ways of embalming they say is that of him whose name I think it impiety to mention when speaking of a matter of such a kind; the second which they show is less good than this and also less expensive; and the third is the least expensive of all. Having told them about this, they inquire of them in which way they desire the corpse of their friend to be prepared. Then they after they have agreed for a certain price depart out of the way, and the others being left behind in the buildings embalm according to the best of these ways thus:--First with the crooked iron tool they draw out the brain through the nostrils, extracting it partly thus and partly by pouring in drugs; and after this with a sharp stone of Ethiopia they make a cut along the side and take out the whole contents of the belly, and when they have cleared out the cavity and cleansed it with palm-wine they cleanse it again with spices pounded up: then they fill the belly with pure myrrh pounded up and with cassia and other spices except frankincense, and sew it together again. Having so done they keep it for embalming covered up in natron for seventy days, but for a longer time than this it is not permitted to embalm it; and when the seventy days are past, they wash the corpse and roll its whole body up in fine linen cut into bands, smearing these beneath with gum, which the Egyptians use generally instead of glue. Then the kinsfolk receive it from them and have a wooden figure made in the shape of a man, and when they have had this made they enclose the corpse, and having shut it up within, they store it then in a sepulchral chamber, setting it to stand upright against the wall. Thus they deal with the corpses which are prepared in the most costly way; but for those who desire the middle way and wish to avoid great cost they prepare the corpse as follows:-- having filled their syringes with the oil which is got from cedar- wood, with this they forthwith fill the belly of the corpse, and this they do without having either cut it open or taken out the bowels, but they inject the oil by the breech, and having stopped the drench from returning back they keep it then the appointed number of days for embalming, and on the last of the days they let the cedar oil come out from the belly, which they before put in; and it has such power that it brings out with it the bowels and interior organs of the body dissolved; and the natron dissolves the flesh, so that there is left of the corpse only the skin and the bones. When they have done this they give back the corpse at once in that condition without working upon it any more. The third kind of embalming, by which are prepared the bodies of those who have less means, is as follows:--they cleanse out the belly with a purge and then keep the body for embalming during the seventy days, and at once after that they give it back to the bringers to carry away. The wives of men of rank when they die are not given at once to be embalmed, nor such women as are very beautiful or of greater regard than others, but on the third or fourth day after their death (and not before) they are delivered to the embalmers. They do so about this matter in order that the embalmers may not abuse their women, for they say that one of them was taken once doing so to the corpse of a woman lately dead, and his fellow-craftsman gave information. Whenever any one, either of the Egyptians themselves or of strangers, is found to have been carried off by a crocodile or brought to his death by the river itself, the people of any city by which he may have been cast up on land must embalm him and lay him out in the fairest way they can and bury him in a sacred burial-place, nor may any of his relations or friends besides touch him, but the priests of the Nile themselves handle the corpse and bury it as that of one who was something more than man.

Hellenic usages they will by no means follow, and to speak generally they follow those of no other men whatever. This rule is observed by most of the Egyptians; but there is a large city named Chemmis in the Theban district near Neapolis, and in this city there is a temple of Perseus the son of Danae which is of a square shape, and round it grow date-palms: the gateway of the temple is built of stone and of very great size, and at the entrance of it stand two great statues of stone. Within this enclosure is a temple-house and in it stands an image of Perseus. These people of Chemmis say that Perseus is wont often to appear in their land and often within the temple, and that a sandal which has been worn by him is found sometimes, being in length two cubits, and whenever this appears all Egypt prospers. This they say, and they do in honour of Perseus after Hellenic fashion thus,-- they hold an athletic contest, which includes the whole list of games, and they offer in prizes cattle and cloaks and skins: and when I inquired why to them alone Perseus was wont to appear, and wherefore they were separated from all the other Egyptians in that they held an athletic contest, they said that Perseus had been born of their city, for Danaos and Lynkeus were men of Chemmis and had sailed to Hellas, and from them they traced a descent and came down to Perseus: and they told me that he had come to Egypt for the reason which the Hellenes also say, namely to bring from Libya the Gorgon's head, and had then visited them also and recognised all his kinsfolk, and they said that he had well learnt the name of Chemmis before he came to Egypt, since he had heard it from his mother, and that they celebrated an athletic contest for him by his own command.

All these are customs practised by the Egyptians who dwell above the fens: and those who are settled in the fenland have the same customs for the most part as the other Egyptians, both in other matters and also in that they live each with one wife only, as do the Hellenes; but for economy in respect of food they have invented these things besides:--when the river has become full and the plains have been flooded, there grow in the water great numbers of lilies, which the Egyptians call *lotos*; these they cut with a sickle and dry in the sun, and then they pound that which grows in the middle of the lotos and which is like the head of a poppy, and they make of it loaves baked with fire. The root also of this lotos is edible and has a rather sweet taste: it

36

is round in shape and about the size of an apple. There are other lilies too, in flower resembling roses, which also grow in the river, and from them the fruit is produced in a separate vessel springing from the root by the side of the plant itself, and very nearly resembles a wasp's comb: in this there grow edible seeds in great numbers of the size of an olive-stone, and they are eaten either fresh or dried. Besides this they pull up from the fens the papyrus which grows every year, and the upper parts of it they cut off and turn to other uses, but that which is left below for about a cubit in length they eat or sell: and those who desire to have the papyrus at its very best bake it in an oven heated red-hot, and then eat it. Some too of these people live on fish alone, which they dry in the sun after having caught them and taken out the entrails, and then when they are dry, they use them for food.

Fish which swim in shoals are not much produced in the rivers, but are bred in the lakes, and they do as follows:--When there comes upon them the desire to breed, they swim out in shoals towards the sea; and the males lead the way shedding forth their milt as they go, while the females, coming after and swallowing it up, from it become impregnated: and when they have become full of young in the sea they swim up back again, each shoal to its own haunts. The same however no longer lead the way as before, but the lead comes now to the females, and they leading the way in shoals do just as the males did, that is to say they shed forth their eggs by a few grains at a time, and the males coming after swallow them up. Now these grains are fish, and from the grains which survive and are not swallowed, the fish grow which afterwards are bred up. Now those of the fish which are caught as they swim out towards the sea are found to be rubbed on the left side of the head, but those which are caught as they swim up again are rubbed on the right side. This happens to them because as they swim down to the sea they keep close to the land on the left side of the river, and again as they swim up they keep to the same side, approaching and touching the bank as much as they can, for fear doubtless of straying from their course by reason of the stream. When the Nile begins to swell, the hollow places of the land and the depressions by the side of the river first begin to fill, as the water soaks through from the river, and so soon as they become full of water, at once they are all filled with little fishes; and whence these are in all likelihood produced, I think that I perceive. In the preceding year, when the Nile goes down, the fish first lay eggs in the mud and then retire with the last of the retreating waters; and when the time comes round again, and the water once more comes over the land, from these eggs forthwith are produced the fishes of which I speak.

Thus it is as regards the fish. And for anointing those of the Egyptians who dwell in the fens use oil from the castor-berry, which oil the Egyptians call *kiki*, and thus they do:--they sow along the banks of the rivers and pools these plants, which in a wild form grow of themselves in the land of the Hellenes; these are sown in Egypt and produce berries in great quantity but of an evil smell; and when they have gathered these some cut them up and press the oil from them, others again roast them first and then boil them down and collect that which runs away from them. The oil is fat and not less suitable for burning than olive-oil, but it gives forth a disagreeable smell. Against the gnats, which are very abundant, they have contrived as follows:--those who dwell above the fen-land are helped by the towers, to which they ascend when they go to rest; for the gnats by reason of the winds are not able to fly up high: but those who dwell in the fen- land have contrived another way instead of the towers, and this it is: --every man of them has got a casting net, with which by day he catches fish, but in the night he uses it for this purpose, that is to say he puts the casting-net round about the bed in which he sleeps, and then creeps in under it and goes to sleep: and the gnats, if he sleeps rolled up in a garment or a linen sheet, bite through these, but through the net they do not even attempt to bite.

Their boats with which they carry cargoes are made of the thorny acacia, of which the form is very like that of the Kyrenian lotos, and that which exudes from it is gum. From this tree they cut pieces of wood about two cubits in length and arrange them like bricks, fastening the boat together by running a great number of long bolts through the two-cubits pieces; and when they have thus fastened the boat together, they lay cross-pieces over the top, using no ribs for the sides; and within they caulk the seams with papyrus. They make one steering-oar for it, which is passed through the bottom of the boat; and they have a mast of acacia and sails of papyrus. These boats cannot sail up the river unless there be a very fresh wind blowing, but are towed from the shore: down-stream however they travel as follows:--they have a door-shaped crate made of tamarisk wood and reed mats sewn together, and also a stone of about two talents weight bored with a hole; and of these the boatman lets the crate float on in front of the boat, fastened with a rope, and the stone drags behind by another rope. The crate then, as the force of the stream presses upon it, goes on swiftly and draws on the *baris* (for so these boats are called), while the stone dragging after it behind and sunk deep in the water keeps its course straight. These boats they have in great numbers and some of them carry many thousands of talents' burden.

When the Nile comes over the land, the cities alone are seen rising above the water, resembling more nearly than anything else the islands in the Egean Sea; for the rest of Egypt becomes a sea and the cities alone rise above water. Accordingly, whenever this happens, they pass by water not now by the channels of the river but over the midst of the plain: for example, as one sails up from Naucratis to Memphis the passage is then close by the pyramids, whereas the usual passage is not the same even here, but goes by the point of the Delta and

38

the city of Kercasoros; while if you sail over the plain to Naucratis from the sea and from Canobos, you will go by Anthylla and the city called after Archander. Of these Anthylla is a city of note and is especially assigned to the wife of him who reigns over Egypt, to supply her with sandals, (this is the case since the time when Egypt came to be under the Persians): the other city seems to me to have its name from Archander the son-in-law of Danaos, who was the son of Phthios, the son of Achaios; for it is called the City of Archander. There might indeed by another Archander, but in any case the name is not Egyptian.

CHAPTER 4

Hitherto my own observation and judgment and inquiry are the vouchers for that which I have said; but from this point onwards I am about to tell the history of Egypt according to that which I have heard, to which will be added also something of that which I have myself seen.

Of Min, who first became king of Egypt, the priests said that on the one hand he banked off the site of Memphis from the river: for the whole stream of the river used to flow along by the sandy mountain-range on the side of Libya, but Min formed by embankments that bend of the river which lies to the South about a hundred furlongs above Memphis, and thus he dried up the old stream and conducted the river so that it flowed in the middle between the mountains: and even now this bend of the Nile is by the Persians kept under very careful watch, that it may flow in the channel to which it is confined, and the bank is repaired every year; for if the river should break through and overflow in this direction, Memphis would be in danger of being overwhelmed by flood. When this Min, who first became king, had made into dry land the part which was dammed off, on the one hand, I say, he founded in it that city which is now called Memphis; for Memphis too is in the narrow part of Egypt; and outside the city he dug round it on the North and West a lake communicating with the river, for the side towards the East is barred by the Nile itself. Then secondly he established in the city the temple of Hephaistos a great work and most worthy of mention. After this man the priests enumerated to me from a papyrus roll the names of other kings, three hundred and thirty in number; and in all these generations of men eighteen were Ethiopians, one was a woman, a native Egyptian, and the rest were men and of Egyptian race: and the name of the woman who reigned was the same as that of the Babylonian queen, namely Nitocris. Of her they said that desiring to take vengeance for her brother, whom the Egyptians had slain when he was their king and then, after having slain him, had given his kingdom to her,--desiring, I say, to take vengeance for him, she destroyed by craft many of the Egyptians. For she caused to be constructed a very large chamber under ground, and making as though she would handsel it but in her mind devising other things, she invited those of the Egyptians whom she knew to have had most part in the murder, and gave a great banquet. Then while they were feasting, she let in the river upon them by a secret conduit of large size. Of her they told no more than this, except that, when this had been accomplished, she threw herself into a room full of embers, in order that she might escape vengeance. As for the other kings, they could tell me of no great works which had been produced by them, and they said that they had no renown except only the last of them, Moiris: he (they said) produced as a memorial of himself the gateway of the temple of Hephaistos which is turned towards the North Wind, and dug a lake, about which I shall set forth afterwards how many furlongs of circuit it has, and in it built pyramids of the size which I shall mention at the same time when I speak of the lake itself. He, they said, produced these works, but of the rest none produced any.

Therefore passing these by I will make mention of the king who came after these, whose name is Sesostris. He (the priests said) first of all set out with ships of war from the Arabian gulf and subdued those who dwelt by the shores of the Erythraian Sea, until as he sailed he came to a sea which could no further be navigated by reason of shoals: then secondly, after he had returned to Egypt, according to the report of the priests he took a great army and marched over the continent, subduing every nation which stood in his way: and those of them whom he found valiant and fighting desperately for their freedom, in their lands he set up pillars which told by inscriptions his own name and the name of his country, and how he had subdued them by his power; but as to those of whose cities he obtained possession without fighting or with ease, on their pillars he inscribed words after the same tenor as he did for the nations which had shown themselves courageous, and in addition he drew upon them the hidden parts of a woman, desiring to signify by this that the people were cowards and effeminate. Thus doing he traversed the continent, until at last he passed over to Europe from Asia and subdued the Scythians and also the Thracians. These, I am of opinion, were the furthest people to which the Egyptian army came, for in their country the pillars are found to have been set up, but in the land beyond this they are no longer found. From this point he turned and began to go back; and when he came to the river Phasis, what happened then I cannot say for certain, whether the king Sesostris himself divided off a certain portion of his army and left the men there as settlers in the land, or whether some of his soldiers were wearied by his distant marches and remained by the river Phasis. For the people of Colchis are evidently Egyptian, and this I perceived for myself before I heard it from others. So when I had come to consider the matter I asked them both; and the Colchians had remembrance of the Egyptians more than the Egyptians of the Colchians; but the Egyptians said they believed that the Colchians were a portion of the army of Sesostris. That this was so I conjectured myself not only because they are dark-skinned and have curly hair (this of itself amounts to nothing, for there are other races which are so), but also still more because the Colchians, Egyptians, and Ethiopians alone of all the races of men have practised circumcision from the first. The Phenicians and the Syrians who dwell in Palestine confess themselves that they have learnt it from the Egyptians, and the Syrians about the river Thermodon and the river Parthenios, and the Macronians, who are their neighbors, say that they have learnt it lately from the Colchians. These are the only races of men who practise circumcision, and these evidently practise it in the same manner as the

Egyptians. Of the Egyptians themselves however and the Ethiopians, I am not able to say which learnt from the other, for undoubtedly it is a most ancient custom; but that the other nations learnt it by intercourse with the Egyptians, this among others is to me a strong proof, namely that those of the Phenicians who have intercourse with Hellas cease to follow the example of the Egyptians in this matter, and do not circumcise their children. Now let me tell another thing about the Colchians to show how they resemble the Egyptians:--they alone work flax in the same fashion as the Egyptians, and the two nations are like one another in their whole manner of living and also in their language: now the linen of Colchis is called by the Hellenes Sardonic, whereas that from Egypt is called Egyptian. The pillars which Sesostris king of Egypt set up in the various countries are for the most part no longer to be seen extant; but in Syria Palestine I myself saw them existing with the inscription upon them which I have mentioned and the emblem. Moreover in Ionia there are two figures of this man carved upon rocks, one on the road by which one goes from the land of Ephesos to Phocaia, and the other on the road from Sardis to Smyrna. In each place there is a figure of a man cut in the rock, of four cubits and a span in height, holding in his right hand a spear and in his left a bow and arrows, and the other equipment which he has is similar to this, for it is both Egyptian and Ethiopian: and from the one shoulder to the other across the breast runs an inscription carved in sacred Egyptian characters, saying thus, "This land with my shoulders I won for myself." But who he is and from whence, he does not declare in these places, though in other places he had declared this. Some of those who have seen these carvings conjecture that the figure is that of Memnon, but herein they are very far from the truth.

As this Egyptian Sesostris was returning and bringing back many men of the nations whose lands he had subdued, when he came (said the priests) to Daphnai in the district of Pelusion on his journey home, his brother to whom Sesostris had entrusted the charge of Egypt invited him and with him his sons to a feast; and then he piled the house round with brushwood and set it on fire: and Sesostris when he discovered this forthwith took counsel with his wife, for he was bringing with him (they said) his wife also; and she counselled him to lay out upon the pyre two of his sons, which were six in number, and so to make a bridge over the burning mass, and that they passing over their bodies should thus escape. This, they said, Sesostris did, and two of his sons were burnt to death in this manner, but the rest got away safe with their father. Then Sesostris, having returned to Egypt and having taken vengeance on his brother employed the multitude which he had brought in of those who whose lands he had subdued, as follows: --these were they drew the stones which in the reign of this king were brought to the temple of Hephaistos, being of very good size; and also these were compelled to dig all the channels

43

which now are in Egypt; and thus (having no such purpose) they caused Egypt, which before was all fit for riding and driving, to be no longer fit for this from thenceforth: for from that time forward Egypt, though it is plain land, has become all unfit for riding and driving, and the cause has been these channels, which are many and run in all directions. But the reason why the king cut up the land was this, namely because those of the Egyptians who had their cities not on the river but in the middle of the country, being in want of water when the river went down from them, found their drink brackish because they had it from wells. For this reason Egypt was cut up: and they said that this king distributed the land to all the Egyptians, giving an equal square portion to each man, and from this he made his revenue, having appointed them to pay a certain rent every year: and if the river should take away anything from any man's portion, he would come to the king and declare that which had happened, and the king used to send men to examine and to find out by measurement how much less the piece of land had become, in order that for the future the man might pay less, in proportion to the rent appointed: and I think that thus the art of geometry was found out and afterwards came into Hellas also. For as touching the sun-dial and the gnomon and the twelve divisions of the day, they were learnt by the Hellenes from the Babylonians. He moreover alone of all the Egyptian kings had rule over Ethiopia; and he left as memorials of himself in front of the temple of Hephaistos two stone statues of thirty cubits each, representing himself and his wife, and others of twenty cubits each representing his four sons: and long afterwards the priest of Hephaistos refused to permit Dareios the Persian to set up a statue of himself in front of them, saying that deeds had not been done by him equal to those which were done by Sesostris the Egyptian; for Sesostris had subdued other nations besides, not fewer than he, and also the Scythians; but Dareios had not been able to conquer the Scythians: wherefore it was not just that he should set up a statue in front of those which Sesostris had dedicated, if he did not surpass him in his deeds. Which speech, they say, Dareios took in good part.

Now after Sesostris had brought his life to an end, his son Pheros, they told me, received in succession the kingdom, and he made no warlike expedition, and moreover it chanced to him to become blind by reason of the following accident:--when the river had come down in flood rising to a height of eighteen cubits, higher than ever before that time, and had gone over the fields, a wind fell upon it and the river became agitated by waves: and this king (they say) moved by presumptuous folly took a spear and cast it into the midst of the eddies of the stream; and immediately upon this he had a disease of the eyes and was by it made blind. For ten years then he was blind, and in the eleventh year there came to him an oracle from the city of Buto saying that the time of his punishment had expired, and that he should see again if he washed his eyes with the water of a woman who had accompanied with

44

her own husband only and had not had knowledge of other men: and first he made trial of his own wife, and then, as he continued blind, he went on to try all the women in turn; and when he had at least regained his sight he gathered together all the women of whom he had made trial, excepting her by whose means he had regained his sight, to one city which now is named Erythrabolos, and having gathered them to this he consumed them all by fire, as well as the city itself; but as for her by whose means he had regained his sight, he had her himself to wife. Then after he had escaped the malady of his eyes he dedicated offerings at each one of the temples which were of renown, and especially (to mention only that which is most worthy of mention) he dedicated at the temple of the Sun works which are worth seeing, namely two obelisks of stone, each of a single block, measuring in length a hundred cubits each one and in breadth eight cubits.

After him, they said, there succeeded to the throne a man of Memphis, whose name in the tongue of the Hellenes was Proteus; for whom there is now a sacred enclosure at Memphis, very fair and well ordered, lying on that side of the temple of Hephaistos which faces the North Wind. Round about this enclosure dwell Phenicians of Tyre, and this whole region is called the Camp of the Tyrians. Within the enclosure of Proteus there is a temple called the temple of the "foreign Aphrodite," which temple I conjecture to be one of Helen the daughter of Tyndareus, not only because I have heard the tale how Helen dwelt with Proteus, but also especially because it is called by the name of the "foreign Aphrodite," for the other temples of Aphrodite which there are have none of them the addition of the word "foreign" to the name.

And the priests told me, when I inquired, that the things concerning Helen happened thus:--Alexander having carried off Helen was sailing away from Sparta to his own land, and when he had come to the Egean Sea contrary winds drove him from his course to the Sea of Egypt; and after that, since the blasts did not cease to blow, he came to Egypt itself, and in Egypt to that which is now named the Canobic mouth of the Nile and to Taricheiai. Now there was upon the shore, as still there is now, a temple of Heracles, in which if any man's slave take refuge and have the sacred marks set upon him, giving himself over to the god, it is not lawful to lay hands upon him; but this custom has continued still unchanged from the beginning down to my own time. Accordingly the attendants of Alexander, having heard of the custom which existed about the temple, ran away from him, and sitting down as suppliants of the god, accused Alexander, because they desired to do him hurt, telling the whole tale how things were about Helen and about the wrong done to Menalaos; and this accusation they made not only to the priests but also to the warden of this river-mouth, whose name was Thonis. Thonis then having heard their tale sent forthwith a message to Proteus at Memphis, which said as follows: "There hath

45

come a stranger, a Teucrian by race, who hath done in Hellas an unholy deed; for he hath deceived the wife of his own host, and is come hither bringing with him this woman herself and very much wealth, having been carried out of his way by winds to thy land. Shall we then allow him to sail out unharmed, or shall we first take away from him that which he brought with him?" In reply to this Proteus sent back a messenger who said thus: "Seize this man, whosoever he may be, who has done impiety to his own host, and bring him away into my presence that I may know what he will find to say." Hearing this, Thonis seized Alexander and detained his ships, and after that he brought the man himself up to Memphis and with him Helen and the wealth he had, and also in addition to them the suppliants. So when all had been conveyed up thither, Proteus began to ask Alexander who he was and from whence he was voyaging; and he both recounted to him his descent and told him the name of his native land, and moreover related of his voyage, from whence he was sailing. After this Proteus asked him whence he had taken Helen; and when Alexander went astray n his account and did not speak the truth, those who had become suppliants convicted him of falsehood, relating in full the whole tale of the wrong done. At length Proteus declared to them this sentence, saying, "Were it not that I count it a matter of great moment not to slay any of those strangers who being driven from their course by winds have come to my land hitherto, I should have taken vengeance on thee on behalf of the man of Hellas, seeing that thou, most base of men, having received from him hospitality, didst work against him a most impious deed. For thou didst go in to the wife of thine own host; and even this was not enough for thee, but thou didst stir her up with desire and hast gone away with her like a thief. Moreover not even this by itself was enough for thee, but thou art come hither with plunder taken from the house of thy host. Now therefore depart, seeing that I have counted it of great moment not to be a slayer of strangers. This woman indeed and the wealth which thou hast I will not allow thee to carry away, but I shall keep them safe for the Hellene who was thy host, until he come himself and desire to carry them off to his home; to thyself however and thy fellow-voyagers I proclaim that ye depart from your anchoring within three days and go from my land to some other; and if not, that ye will be dealt with as enemies."

This the priests said was the manner of Helen's coming to Proteus; and I suppose that Homer also had heard this story, but since it was not so suitable to the composition of his poem as the other which he followed, he dismissed it finally, making it clear at the same time that he was acquainted with that story also: and according to the manner in which he described the wanderings of Alexander in the Iliad (nor did he elsewhere retract that which he had said) of his course, wandering to various lands, and that he came among other places to Sidon in Phenicia. Of this the poet has made mention in the "prowess of Diomede," and the verses run thus:

46

"There she had robes many-coloured, the works of women of Sidon,
Those whom her son himself the god-like of form Alexander   Carried
from Sidon, what time the broad sea-path he sailed over   Bringing back
Helene home, of a noble father begotten."

And in the Odyssey also he has made mention of it in these verses:

"Such had the daughter of Zeus, such drugs of exquisite cunning,
Good, which to her the wife of Thon, Polydamna, had given,
Dwelling in Egypt, the land where the bountiful meadow produces
Drugs more than all lands else, many good being mixed, many evil."

And thus too Menelaos says to Telemachos:

"Still the gods stayed me in Egypt, to come back hither desiring,
Stayed me from voyaging home, since sacrifice due I performed not."

In these lines he makes it clear that he knew of the wanderings
of Alexander to Egypt, for Syria borders upon Egypt and the
Phenicians, of whom is Sidon, dwell in Syria. By these lines and by this
passage it is also most clearly shown that the "Cyprian Epic" was not
written by Homer but by some other man: for in this it is said that on
the third day after leaving Sparta Alexander came to Ilion bringing
with him Helen, having had a "gently-blowing wind and a smooth
sea," whereas in the Iliad it says that he wandered from his course
when he brought her.

Let us now leave Homer and the "Cyprian Epic"; but this I will
say, namely that I asked the priests whether it is but an idle tale
which the Hellenes tell of that which they say happened about Ilion;
and they answered me thus, saying that they had their knowledge
by inquiries from Menelaos himself. After the rape of Helen there
came indeed, they said, to the Teucrian land a large army of Hellenes
to help Menelaos; and when the army had come out of the ships to land
and had pitched its camp there, they sent messengers to Ilion, with
whom went also Menelaos himself; and when these entered within the
wall they demanded back Helen and the wealth which Alexander had
stolen from Menelaos and had taken away; and moreover they
demanded satisfaction for the wrongs done: and the Teucrians told the
same tale then and afterwards, both with oath and without oath, namely
that in deed and in truth they had not Helen nor the wealth for which
demand was made, but that both were in Egypt; and that they could not
justly be compelled to give satisfaction for that which Proteus the king
of Egypt had. The Hellenes however thought that they were being
mocked by them and besieged the city, until at last they took it; and
when they had taken the wall and did not find Helen, but heard the
same tale as before, then they believed the former tale and sent

Menelaos himself to Proteus. And Menelaos having come to Egypt and having sailed up to Memphis, told the truth of these matters, and not only found great entertainment, but also received Helen unhurt, and all his own wealth besides. Then, however, after he had been thus dealt with, Menelaos showed himself ungrateful to the Egyptians; for when he set forth to sail away, contrary winds detained him, and as this condition of things lasted long, he devised an impious deed; for he took two children of natives and made sacrifice of them. After this, when it was known that he had done so, he became abhorred, and being pursued he escaped and got away in his ships to Libya; but whither he went besides after this, the Egyptians were not able to tell. Of these things they said that they found out part by inquiries, and the rest, namely that which happened in their own land, they related from sure and certain knowledge.

Thus the priests of the Egyptians told me; and I myself also agree with the story which was told of Helen, adding this consideration, namely that if Helen had been in Ilion she would have been given up to the Hellenes, whether Alexander consented or no; for Priam assuredly was not so mad, nor yet the others of his house, that they were desirous to run risk of ruin for themselves and their children and their city, in order that Alexander might have Helen as his wife: and even supposing that during the first part of the time they had been so inclined, yet when many others of the Trojans besides were losing their lives as often as they fought with the Hellenes, and of the sons of Priam himself always two or three or even more were slain when a battle took place (if one may trust at all to the Epic poets),--when, I say, things were coming thus to pass, I consider that even if Priam himself had had Helen as his wife, he would have given her back to the Achaians, if at least by so doing he might be freed from the evils which oppressed him. Nor even was the kingdom coming to Alexander next, so that when Priam was old the government was in his hands; but Hector, who was both older and more of a man than he, would certainly have received it after the death of Priam; and him it behoved not to allow his brother to go on with his wrong-doing, considering that great evils were coming to pass on his account both to himself privately and in general to the other Trojans. In truth however they lacked the power to give Helen back; and the Hellenes did not believe them, though they spoke the truth; because, as I declare my opinion, the divine power was purposing to cause them utterly to perish, and so make it evident to men that for great wrongs great also are the chastisements which come from the gods. And thus have I delivered my opinion concerning these matters.

After Proteus, they told me, Rhampsinitos received in succession the kingdom, who left as a memorial of himself that gateway to the temple of Hephaistos which is turned towards the West, and in front of the gateway he set up two statues, in height five-and-twenty cubits, of which the one which stands on the North side is called by

the Egyptians Summer and the one on the South side Winter; and to
that one which they call Summer they do reverence and make offerings,
while to the other which is called Winter they do the opposite of these
things. This king, they said, got great wealth of silver, which none of
the kings born after him could surpass or even come near to; and
wishing to store his wealth in safety he caused to be built a chamber
of stone, one of the walls whereof was towards the outside of his
palace: and the builder of this, having a design against it, contrived
as follows, that is, he disposed one of the stones in such a manner
that it could be taken out easily from the wall either by two men or
even by one. So when the chamber was finished, the king stored his
money in it, and after some time the builder, being near the end of his
life, called to him his sons (for he had two) and to them he related how
he had contrived in building the treasury of the king, and all
in forethought for them, that they might have ample means of living.
And when he had clearly set forth to them everything concerning the
taking out of the stone, he gave them the measurements, saying that if
they paid heed to this matter they would be stewards of the
king's treasury. So he ended his life, and his sons made no long delay
in setting to work, but went to the palace by night, and having found
the stone in the wall of the chamber they dealt with it easily and
carried forth for themselves great quantity of the wealth within. And the
king happening to open the chamber, he marvelled when he saw the
vessels falling short of the full amount, and he did not know on whom
he should lay the blame, since the seals were unbroken and the
chamber had been close shut; but when upon his opening the chamber
a second and a third time the money was each time seen to be
diminished, for the thieves did not slacken in their assaults upon it, he
did as follows:--having ordered traps to be made he set these round
about the vessels in which the money was; and when the thieves had
come as at former times and one of them had entered, then so soon as
he came near to one of the vessels he was straightway caught in the
trap: and when he perceived in what evil case he was, straightway
calling his brother he showed him what the matter was, and bade him
enter as quickly as possible and cut off his head, for fear lest being seen
and known he might bring about the destruction of his brother also. And
to the other it seemed that he spoke well, and he was persuaded and
did so; and fitting the stone into its place he departed home bearing
with him the head of his brother. Now when it became day, the king
entered into the chamber and was very greatly amazed, seeing the body
of the thief held in the trap without his head, and the chamber
unbroken, with no way to come in by or go out: and being at a loss he
hung up the dead body of the thief upon the wall and set guards there,
with charge if they saw any one weeping or bewailing himself to seize
him and bring him before the king. And when the dead body had been
hung up, the mother was greatly grieved, and speaking with the son
who survived she enjoined him, in whatever way he could, to contrive
means by which he might take down and bring home the body of his

49

brother; and if he should neglect to do this, she earnestly threatened that she would go and give information to the king that he had the money. So as the mother dealt hardly with the surviving son, and he though saying many things to her did not persuade her, he contrived for his purpose a device as follows:--Providing himself with asses he filled some skins with wine and laid them upon the asses, and after that he drove them along: and when he came opposite to those who were guarding the corpse hung up, he drew towards him two or three of the necks of the skins and loosened the cords with which they were tied. Then when the wine was running out, he began to beat his head and cry out loudly, as if he did not know to which of the asses he should first turn; and when the guards saw the wine flowing out in streams, they ran together to the road with drinking vessels in their hands and collected the wine that was poured out, counting it so much gain; and he abused them all violently, making as if he were angry, but when the guards tried to appease him, after a time he feigned to be pacified and to abate his anger, and at length he drove his asses out of the road and began to set their loads right. Then more talk arose among them, and one or two of them made jests at him and brought him to laugh with them; and in the end he made them a present of one of the skins in addition to what they had. Upon that they lay down there without more ado, being minded to drink, and they took him into their company and invited him to remain with them and join them in their drinking: so he (as may be supposed) was persuaded and stayed. Then as they in their drinking bade him welcome in a friendly manner, he made a present to them also of another of the skins; and so at length having drunk liberally the guards became completely intoxicated; and being overcome by sleep they went to bed on the spot where they had been drinking. He then, as it was now far on in the night, first took down the body of his brother, and then in mockery shaved the right cheeks of all the guards; and after that he put the dead body upon the asses and drove them away home, having accomplished that which was enjoined him by his mother. Upon this the king, when it was reported to him that the dead body of the thief had been stolen away, displayed great anger; and desiring by all means that it should be found out who it might be who devised these things, did this (so at least they said, but I do not believe the account),--he caused his own daughter to sit in the stews, and enjoined her to receive all equally, and before having commerce with any one to compel him to tell her what was the most cunning and what the most unholy deed which had been done by him in all his life-time; and whosoever should relate that which had happened about the thief, him she must seize and not let him go out. Then as she was doing that which was enjoined by her father, the thief, hearing for what purpose this was done and having a desire to get the better of the king in resource, did thus:--from the body of one lately dead he cut off the arm at the shoulder and went with it under his mantle: and having gone in to the daughter of the king, and being asked that which the others also were asked, he related that he had done the most unholy

50

deed when he cut off the head of his brother, who had been caught in a trap in the king's treasure-chamber, and the most cunning deed in that he made drunk the guards and took down the dead body of his brother hanging up; and she when she heard it tried to take hold of him, but the thief held out to her in the darkness the arm of the corpse, which she grasped and held, thinking that she was holding the arm of the man himself; but the thief left it in her hands and departed, escaping through the door. Now when this also was reported to the king, he was at first amazed at the ready invention and daring of the fellow, and then afterwards he sent round to all the cities and made proclamation granting a free pardon to the thief, and also promising a great reward if he would come into his presence. The thief accordingly trusting to the proclamation came to the king, and Rhampsinitos greatly marvelled at him, and gave him this daughter of his to wife, counting him to be the most knowing of all men; for as the Egyptians were distinguished from all other men, so was he from the other Egyptians.

After these things they said this king went down alive to that place which by the Hellenes is called Hades, and there played at dice with Demeter, and in some throws he overcame her and in others he was overcome by her; and he came back again having as a gift from her a handkerchief of gold: and they told me that because of the going down of Rhampsinitos the Egyptians after he came back celebrated a feast, which I know of my own knowledge also that they still observe even to my time; but whether it is for this cause that they keep the feast or for some other, I am not able to say. However, the priests weave a robe completely on the very day of the feast, and forthwith they bind up the eyes of one of them with a fillet, and having led him with the robe to the way by which one goes to the temple of Demeter, they depart back again themselves. This priest, they say, with his eyes bound up is led by two wolves to the temple of Demeter, which is distant from the city twenty furlongs, and then afterwards the wolves lead him back again from the temple to the same spot. Now as to the tales told by the Egyptians, any man may accept them to whom such things appear credible; as for me, it is to be understood throughout the whole of the history that I write by hearsay that which is reported by the people in each place. The Egyptians say that Demeter and Dionysos are rulers of the world below; and the Egyptians are also the first who reported the doctrine that the soul of man is immortal, and that when the body dies, the soul enters into another creature which chances then to be coming to the birth, and when it has gone the round of all the creatures of land and sea and of the air, it enters again into a human body as it comes to the birth; and that it makes this round in a period of three thousand years. This doctrine certain Hellenes adopted, some earlier and some later, as if it were of their own invention, and of these men I know the names but I abstain from recording them.

51

Down to the time when Rhampsinitos was king, they told me there was in Egypt nothing but orderly rule, and Egypt prospered greatly; but after him Cheops became king over them and brought them to every kind of evil: for he shut up all the temples, and having first kept them from sacrifices there, he then bade all the Egyptians work for him. So some were appointed to draw stones from the stone-quarries in the Arabian mountains to the Nile, and others he ordered to receive the stones after they had been carried over the river in boats, and to draw them to those which are called the Libyan mountains; and they worked by a hundred thousand men at a time, for each three months continually. Of this oppression there passed ten years while the causeway was made by which they drew the stones, which causeway they built, and it is a work not much less, as it appears to me, than the pyramid; for the length of it is five furlongs and the breadth ten fathoms and the height, where it is highest, eight fathoms, and it is made of stone smoothed and with figures carved upon it. For this they said, the ten years were spent, and for the underground he caused to be made as sepulchral chambers for himself in an island, having conducted thither a channel from the Nile. For the making of the pyramid itself there passed a period of twenty years; and the pyramid is square, each side measuring eight hundred feet, and the height of it is the same. It is built of stone smoothed and fitted together in the most perfect manner, not one of the stones being less than thirty feet in length. This pyramid was made after the manner of steps which some called "rows" and others "bases": and when they had first made it thus, they raised the remaining stones with machines made of short pieces of timber, raising them first from the ground to the first stage of the steps, and when the stone got up to this it was placed upon another machine standing on the first stage, and so from this it was drawn to the second upon another machine; for as many as were the courses of the steps, so many machines there were also, or perhaps they transferred one and the same machine, made so as easily to be carried, to each stage successively, in order that they might take up the stones; for let it be told in both ways, according as it is reported. However that may be the highest parts of it were finished first, and afterwards they proceeded to finish that which came next to them, and lastly they finished the parts of it near the ground and the lowest ranges. On the pyramid it is declared in Egyptian writing how much was spent on radishes and onions and leeks for the workmen, and if I rightly remember that which the interpreter said in reading to me this inscription, a sum of one thousand six hundred talents of silver was spent; and if this is so, how much besides is likely to have been expended upon the iron with which they worked, and upon bread and clothing for the workmen, seeing that they were building the works for the time which has been mentioned and were occupied for no small time besides, as I suppose, in the cutting and bringing of the stones and in working at the excavation under the ground? Cheops moreover came, they said, to such a pitch of wickedness, that being in want of money he caused his own daughter to sit in the stews, and ordered her to obtain from those who came a certain amount of money (how much it was they did not tell me): and she not only obtained the sum appointed by her father, but also she formed a design for herself privately to leave behind her a memorial, and she requested each man who came in to give her one stone upon her building: and of these stones, they told me, the pyramid was built which stands in front of the great pyramid in the middle of the three, each side being one hundred and fifty feet in length.

This Cheops, the Egyptians said, reigned fifty years; and after he was dead his brother Chephren succeeded to the kingdom. This king followed the same manner of dealing as the other, both in all the rest and also in that he made a pyramid, not indeed attaining to the measurements of that which was built by the former (this I know, having myself also measured it), and moreover there are no underground chambers beneath nor does a channel come from the Nile flowing to this one as to the other, in which the water coming through a conduit built for it flows round an island within, where they say that Cheops himself is laid: but for a basement he built the first course of Ethiopian stone of divers colours; and this pyramid he made forty feet lower than the other as regards size, building it close to the great pyramid. These stand both upon the same hill, which is about a hundred feet high. And Chephren they said reigned fifty and six years. Here then they reckon one hundred and six years, during which they say that there was nothing but evil for the Egyptians, and the temples were kept closed and not opened during all that time. These kings the Egyptians by reason of their hatred of them are not very willing to name; nay, they even call the pyramids after the name of Philitis the shepherd, who at that time pastured flocks in those regions. After him, they said, Mykerinos became king over Egypt, who was the son of Cheops; and to him his father's deeds were displeasing, and he both opened the temples and gave liberty to the people, who were ground down to the last extremity of evil, to return to their own business and to their sacrifices: also he gave decisions of their causes juster than those of all the other kings besides. In regard to this then they commend this king more than all the other kings who had arisen in Egypt before him; for he not only gave good decisions, but also when a man complained of the decision, he gave him recompense from his own goods and thus satisfied his desire. But while Mykerinos was acting mercifully to his subjects and practising this conduct which has been said, calamities befell him, of which the first was this, namely that his daughter died, the only child whom he had in his house: and being above measure grieved by that which had befallen him, and desiring to bury his daughter in a manner more remarkable than others, he made a cow of wood, which he covered over with gold, and then within it he buried this daughter who as I said, had died. This cow was not covered up in the ground, but it might be seen even down to my own time in the city of Sais, placed within the royal palace in a chamber which was greatly adorned; and they offer incense of all kinds before it every day, and each night a lamp burns beside it all through the night. Near this cow in another chamber stand images of the concubines of Mykerinos, as the priests at Sais told me; for there are in fact colossal wooden statues, in number about twenty, made with naked bodies; but who they are I am not able to say, except only that which is reported. Some however tell about this cow and the colossal statues the following tale, namely that Mykerinos was enamoured of his own daughter and afterwards ravished her; and upon this they say that the girl strangled herself for grief, and he buried her in this cow; and her mother cut off the hands of the maids who had betrayed the daughter to her father; wherefore now the images of them have suffered that which the maids suffered in their life. In thus saying they speak idly, as it seems to me, especially in what they say about the hands of the statues; for as to this, even we ourselves saw that their hands had dropped off from lapse of time, and they were to be seen still lying at their feet even down to my time. The cow is covered up with a crimson robe, except only the head and the neck, which are seen, overlaid with gold very thickly; and between the horns there is the disc of the sun figured in gold. The cow is not standing up but kneeling, and in size is equal to a large living cow. Every year it is carried forth from the chamber, at those times, I say, the Egyptians beat themselves for that god whom I will not name upon occasion of such a matter; at these times, I say, they also carry forth the cow to the light of day, for they say that she asked of her father Mykerinos, when she was dying, that she might look upon the sun once in the year.

After the misfortune of his daughter it happened, they said, secondly to this king as follows:--An oracle came to him from the city of Buto, saying that he was destined to live but six years more, in the seventh year to end his life: and he being indignant at it sent to the Oracle a reproach against the god, making complaint in reply that whereas his father and uncle, who had shut up the temples and had not only not remembered the gods, but also had been destroyers of men, had lived for a long time, he himself, who practised piety, was destined to end his life so soon: and from the Oracle came a second message, which said that it was for this very cause that he was bringing his life to a swift close; for he had not done that which it was appointed for him to do, since it was destined that Egypt should suffer evils for a hundred and fifty years, and the two kings who had arisen before him had perceived this, but he had not. Mykerinos having heard this, and considering that this sentence had passed upon him beyond recall, procured many lamps, and whenever night came on he lighted these and began to drink and take his pleasure, ceasing neither by day nor by night; and he went about to the fen-country and to the woods and wherever he heard there were the most suitable places of enjoyment. This he devised (having a mind to prove that the Oracle spoke falsely) in order that he might have twelve years of life instead of six, the nights being turned into days.

This king also left behind him a pyramid, much smaller than that of his father, of a square shape and measuring on each side three hundred feet lacking twenty, built moreover of Ethiopian stone up to half the height. This pyramid some of the Hellenes say was built by the courtesan Rhodopis, not therein speaking rightly: and besides this it is evident to me that they who speak thus do not even know who Rhodopis was, for otherwise they would not have attributed to her the building of a pyramid like this, on which have been spent (so to speak) innumerable thousands of talents: moreover they do not know that Rhodopis flourished in the reign of Amasis, and not in this king's reign; for Rhodopis lived very many years later than the kings who left behind them these pyramids. By descent she was of Thrace, and she was a slave of Iadmon the son of Hephaistopolis a Samian, and a fellow-slave of Esop the maker of fables; for he too was once the slave of Iadmon, as was proved especially by this fact, namely that when the people of Delphi repeatedly made proclamation in accordance with an oracle, to find some one who would take up the blood-money for the death of Esop, no one else appeared, but at length the grandson of Iadmon, called Iadmon also, took it up; and thus it is showed that Esop too was the slave of Iadmon. As for Rhodopis, she came to Egypt brought by Xanthes the Samian, and having come thither to exercise her calling she was redeemed from slavery for a great sum by a man of Mytilene, Charaxos son of Scamandronymos and brother of Sappho the lyric poet. Thus was Rhodopis set free, and she remained in Egypt and by her beauty won so much liking that she made great gain of money for one like Rhodopis, though not enough to suffice for the cost of such a pyramid as this. In truth there is no need to ascribe to her very great riches, considering that the tithe of her wealth may still be seen even to this time by any one who desires it: for Rhodopis wished to leave behind her a memorial of herself in Hellas, namely to cause a thing to be made such as happens not to have been thought of or dedicated in a temple by any besides, and to dedicate this at Delphi as a memorial of herself. Accordingly with the tithe of her wealth she caused to be made spits of iron of size large enough to pierce a whole ox, and many in number, going as far therein as her tithe allowed her, and she sent them to Delphi: these are even at the present time lying there, heaped all together behind the altar which the Chians dedicated, and just opposite to the cell of the temple. Now at Naucratis, as it happens, the courtesans are rather apt to win credit; for this woman first, about whom the story to which I refer is told, became so famous that all the Hellenes without exception came to know the name of Rhodopis, and then after her one whose name was Archidiche became a subject of song all over Hellas, though she was less talked of than the other. As for Charaxos, when after redeeming

Rhodopis he returned back to Mytilene, Sappho in an ode violently abused him. Of Rhodopis then I shall say no more.

After Mykerinos the priests said Asychis became king of Egypt, and he made for Hephaistos the temple gateway which is towards the sunrising, by far the most beautiful and the largest of the gateways; for while they all have figures carved upon them and innumerable ornaments of building besides, this has them very much more than the rest. In this king's reign they told me that, as the circulation of money was very slow, a law was made for the Egyptians that a man might have that money lent to him which he needed, by offering as security the dead body of his father; and there was added moreover to this law another, namely that he who lent the money should have a claim also to the whole of the sepulchral chamber belonging to him who received it, and that the man who offered that security should be subject to this penalty, if he refused to pay back the debt, namely that neither the man himself should be allowed to have burial, when he died, either in that family burial-place or in any other, nor should he be allowed to bury any of his kinsmen whom he lost by death. This king desiring to surpass the kings of Egypt who had arisen before him left as a memorial of himself a pyramid which he made of bricks and on it there is an inscription carved in stone and saying thus: "Despise not me in comparison with the pyramids of stone, seeing that I excel them as much as Zeus excels the other gods; for with a pole they struck into the lake, and whatever of the mud attached itself to the pole, this they gathered up and made bricks, and in such manner they finished me."

Such were the deeds which this king performed: and after him reigned a blind man of the city of Anysis, whose name was Anysis.   In his reign the Ethiopians and Sabacos the king of the Ethiopians marched upon Egypt with a great host of men; so this blind man departed, flying to the fen-country, and the Ethiopian was king over Egypt for fifty years, during which he performed deeds as follows:--whenever any man of the Egyptians committed any transgression, he would never put him to death, but he gave sentence upon each man according to the greatness of the wrong-doing, appointing them to work at throwing up an embankment before that city from whence each man came of those who committed wrong. Thus the cities were made higher still than before; for they were embanked first by those who dug the channels in the reign of Sesostris, and then secondly in the reign of the Ethiopian, and thus they were made very high: and while other cities in Egypt also stood high, I think in the town at Bubastis especially the earth was piled up. In this city there is a temple very well worthy of mention, for though there are other temples which are larger and build with more cost, none more than this is a pleasure to the eyes. Now Bubastis in the Hellenic tongue is Artemis, and her temple is ordered thus:--Except the entrance it is completely surrounded by water; for channels come in from the Nile, not joining one another, but each extending as far as the entrance of the temple, one flowing round on the one side and the other on the other side, each a hundred feet broad and shaded over with trees; and the gateway has a height of ten fathoms, and it is adorned with figures six cubits high, very noteworthy. This temple is in the middle of the city and is looked down upon from all sides as one goes round, for since the city has been banked up to a height, while the temple has not been moved from the place where it was at the first built, it is possible to look down into it: and round it runs a stone wall with figures carved upon it, while within it there is a grove of very large trees planted round a large temple-house, within which is the image of the goddess: and the breadth and length of the temple is a furlong every way. Opposite the entrance there is a road paved with stone for about three furlongs, which leads through the market-place towards the East, with a breadth of about four hundred feet; and on this side and on that grow trees of height reaching to heaven: and the road leads to the temple of Hermes. This temple then is thus ordered.

CHAPTER 5

The final deliverance from the Ethiopian came about (they said) as follows:--he fled away because he had seen in his sleep a vision, in which it seemed to him that a man came and stood by him and counselled him to gather together all the priests in Egypt and cut them asunder in the midst. Having seen this dream, he said that it seemed to him that the gods were foreshowing him this to furnish an occasion against him, in order that he might do an impious deed with respect to religion, and so receive some evil either from the gods or from men: he would not however do so, but in truth (he said) the time had expired, during which it had been prophesied to him that he should rule Egypt before he departed thence. For when he was in Ethiopia the Oracles which the Ethiopians consult had told him that it was fated for him to rule Egypt fifty years: since then this time was now expiring, and the vision of the dream also disturbed him, Sabacos departed out of Egypt of his own free will.

Then when the Ethiopian had gone away out of Egypt, the blind man came back from the fen-country and began to rule again, having lived there during fifty years upon an island which he had made by heaping up ashes and earth: for whenever any of the Egyptians visited him bringing food, according as it had been appointed to them severally to do without the knowledge of the Ethiopian, he bade them bring also some ashes for their gift. This island none was able to find before Amyrtaios; that is, for more than seven hundred years the kings who arose before Amyrtaios were not able to find it. Now the name of this island is Elbo, and its size is ten furlongs each way.

After him there came to the throne the priest of Hephaistos, whose name was Sethos. This man, they said, neglected and held in no regard the warrior class of the Egyptians, considering that he would have no need of them; and besides other slights which he put upon them, he also took from them the yokes of corn-land which had been given to them as a special gift in the reigns of the former kings, twelve yokes to each man. After this, Sanacharib king of the Arabians and of the Assyrians marched a great host against Egypt. Then the warriors of the Egyptians refused to come to the rescue, and the priest, being driven into a strait, entered into the sanctuary of the temple and bewailed to the image of the god the danger which was impending over him; and as he was thus lamenting, sleep came upon him, and it seemed to him in his vision that the god came and stood by him and encouraged him, saying that he should suffer no evil if he went forth to meet the army of the Arabians; for he would himself send him helpers. Trusting in these things seen in sleep, he took with him, they said, those of the Egyptians who were willing to follow him, and encamped in

Pelusion, for by this way the invasion came: and not one of the warrior class followed him, but shop-keepers and artisans and men of the market. Then after they came, there swarmed by night upon their enemies mice of the fields, and ate up their quivers and their bows, and moreover the handles of their shields, so that on the next day they fled, and being without defence of arms great numbers fell. And at the present time this king stands in the temple of Hephaistos in stone, holding upon his hand a mouse, and by letters inscribed he says these words: "Let him who looks upon me learn to fear the gods."

So far in the story the Egyptians and the priests were they who made the report, declaring that from the first king down to this priest of Hephaistos who reigned last, there had been three hundred and forty- one generations of men, and that in them there had been the same number of chief-priests and of kings: but three hundred generations of men are equal to ten thousand years, for a hundred years is three generations of men; and in the one-and-forty generations which remain, those I mean which were added to the three hundred, there are one thousand three hundred and forty years. Thus in the period of eleven thousand three hundred and forty years they said that there had arisen no god in human form; nor even before that time or afterwards among the remaining kings who arise in Egypt, did they report that anything of that kind had come to pass. In this time they said that the sun had moved four times from his accustomed place of rising, and where he now sets he had thence twice had his rising, and in the place from whence he now rises he had twice had his setting; and in the meantime nothing in Egypt had been changed from its usual state, neither that which comes from the earth nor that which comes to them from the river nor that which concerns diseases or deaths. And formerly when Hecataios the historian was in Thebes, and had traced his descent and connected his family with a god in the sixteenth generation before, the priests of Zeus did for him much the same as they did for me (though I had not traced my descent). They led me into the sanctuary of the temple, which is of great size, and they counted up the number, showing colossal wooden statues in number the same as they said; for each chief-priest there sets up in his lifetime an image of himself: accordingly the priests, counting and showing me these, declared to me that each one of them was a son succeeding his own father, and they went up through the series of images from the image of the one who had died last, until they had declared this of the whole number. And when Hecataios had traced his descent and connected his family with a god in the sixteenth generation, they traced a descent in opposition to his, besides their numbering, not accepting it from him that a man had been born from a god; and they traced their counter-descent thus, saying that each one of the statues had been /piromis/ son of /piromis/, until they had declared this of the whole three hundred and forty-five statues, each one being surnamed /piromis/; and neither with a god nor a hero did they connect their descent. Now

60

/piromis/ means in the tongue of Hellas "honourable and good man." From their declaration then it followed, that they of whom the images were had been of form like this, and far removed from being gods: but in the time before these men they said that gods were the rulers in Egypt, not mingling with men, and that of these always one had power at a time; and the last of them who was king over Egypt was Oros the son of Osiris, whom the Hellenes call Apollo: he was king over Egypt last, having deposed Typhon. Now Osiris in the tongue of Hellas is Dionysos.

Among the Hellenes Heracles and Dionysos and Pan are accounted the lastest-born of the gods; but with the Egyptians Pan is a very ancient god, and he is one of those which are called eight gods, while Heracles is of the second rank, who are called the twelve gods, and Dionysos is of the third rank, namely of those who were born of the twelve gods. Now as to Heracles I have shown already how many years old he is according to the Egyptians themselves, reckoning down to the reign of Amasis, and Pan is said to have existed for yet more years than these, and Dionysos for the smallest number of years as compared with the others; and even for this last they reckon down to the reign of Amasis fifteen thousand years. This the Egyptians say that they know for a certainty, since they always kept a reckoning and wrote down the years as they came. Now the Dionysos who is said to have been born of Semele the daughter of Cadmos, was born about sixteen hundred years before my time, and Heracles who was the son of Alcmene, about nine hundred years, and that Pan who was born of Penelope, for of her and of Hermes Pan is said by the Hellenes to have been born, came into being later than the wars of Troy, about eight hundred years before my time. Of these two accounts every man may adopt that one which he shall find the more credible when he hears it. I however, for my part, have already declared my opinion about them. For if these also, like Heracles the son of Amphitryon, had appeared before all men's eyes and had lived their lives to old age in Hellas, I mean Dionysos the son of Semele and Pan the son of Penelope, then one would have said that these also had been born mere men, having the names of those gods who had come into being long before: but as it is, with regard to Dionysos the Hellenes say that as soon as he was born Zeus sewed him up in his thigh and carried him to Nysa, which is above Egypt in the land of Ethiopia; and as to Pan, they cannot say whither he went after he was born. Hence it has become clear to me that the Hellenes learnt the names of these gods later than those of the other gods, and trace their descent as if their birth occurred at the time when they first learnt their names.

Thus far then the history is told by the Egyptians themselves; but I will now recount that which other nations also tell, and the Egyptians in agreement with the others, of that which happened in this land:

61

and there will be added to this also something of that which I have
myself seen.

Being set free after the reign of the priest of Hephaistos,
the Egyptians, since they could not live any time without a king, set
up over them twelve kings, having divided all Egypt into twelve
parts. These made intermarriages with one another and reigned,
making agreement that they would not put down one another by force,
nor seek to get an advantage over one another, but would live in
perfect friendship: and the reason why they made these agreements,
guarding them very strongly from violation, was this, namely that an
oracle had been given to them at first when they began to exercise their
rule, that he of them who should pour a libation with a bronze cup in
the temple of Hephaistos, should be king of all Egypt (for they used
to assemble together in all the temples). Moreover they resolved to
join all together and leave a memorial of themselves; and having
so resolved they caused to be made a labyrinth, situated a little
above the lake of Moiris and nearly opposite to that which is called
the City of Crocodiles. This I saw myself, and I found it greater
than words can say. For if one should put together and reckon up all
the buildings and all the great works produced by Hellenes, they
would prove to be inferior in labour and expense to this labyrinth,
though it is true that both the temple at Ephesos and that at Samos are
works worthy of note. The pyramids also were greater than words can
say, and each one of them is equal to many works of the Hellenes, great
as they may be; but the labyrinth surpasses even the pyramids. It has
twelve courts covered in, with gates facing one another, six upon the
North side and six upon the South, joining on one to another, and the
same wall surrounds them all outside; and there are in it two kinds
of chambers, the one kind below the ground and the other above
upon these, three thousand in number, of each kind fifteen hundred.
The upper set of chambers we ourselves saw, going through them, and
we tell of them having looked upon them with our own eyes; but
the chambers under ground we heard about only; for the Egyptians who
had charge of them were not willing on any account to show them,
saying that here were the sepulchres of the kings who had first built
this labyrinth and of the sacred crocodiles. Accordingly we speak of
the chambers below by what we received from hearsay, while those
above we saw ourselves and found them to be works of more than
human greatness. For the passages through the chambers, and the
goings this way and that way through the courts, which were admirably
adorned, afforded endless matter for marvel, as we went through from a
court to the chambers beyond it, and from the chambers to colonnades,
and from the colonnades to other rooms, and then from the chambers
again to other courts. Over the whole of these is a roof made of stone
like the walls; and the walls are covered with figures carved upon them,
each court being surrounded with pillars of white stone fitted
together most perfectly; and at the end of the labyrinth, by the corner

of it, there is a pyramid of forty fathoms, upon which large figures are carved, and to this there is a way made under ground.

Such is this labyrinth: but a cause for marvel even greater than this is afforded by the lake, which is called the lake of Moiris, along the side of which this labyrinth is built. The measure of its circuit is three thousand six hundred furlongs (being sixty *schoines*), and this is the same number of furlongs as the extent of Egypt itself along the sea. The lake lies extended lengthwise from North to South, and in depth where it is deepest it is fifty fathoms. That this lake is artificial and formed by digging is self-evident, for about in the middle of the lake stand two pyramids, each rising above the water to a height of fifty fathoms, the part which is built below the water being of just the same height; and upon each is placed a colossal statue of stone sitting upon a chair. Thus the pyramids are a hundred fathoms high; and these hundred fathoms are equal to a furlong of six hundred feet, the fathom being measured as six feet or four cubits, the feet being four palms each, and the cubits six. The water in the lake does not come from the place where it is, for the country there is very deficient in water, but it has been brought thither from the Nile by a canal; and for six months the water flows into the lake, and for six months out into the Nile again; and whenever it flows out, then for the six months it brings into the royal treasury a talent of silver a day from the fish which are caught, and twenty pounds when the water comes in. The natives of the place moreover said that this lake had an outlet under ground to the Syrtis which is in Libya, turning towards the interior of the continent upon the Western side and running along by the mountain which is above Memphis. Now since I did not see anywhere existing the earth dug out of this excavation (for that was a matter which drew my attention), I asked those who dwelt nearest to the lake where the earth was which had been dug out. These told me to what place it had been carried away; and I readily believed them, for I knew by report that a similar thing had been done at Nineveh, the city of the Assyrians. There certain thieves formed a design once to carry away the wealth of Sardanapallos son of Ninos, the king, which wealth was very great and was kept in treasure-houses under the earth. Accordingly they began from their own dwelling, and making estimate of their direction they dug under ground towards the king's palace; and the earth which was brought out of the excavation they used to carry away, when night came on, to the river Tigris which flows by the city of Nineveh, until at last they accomplished that which they desired. Similarly, as I heard, the digging of the lake in Egypt was effected, except that it was done not by night but during the day; for as they dug the Egyptians carried to the Nile the earth which was dug out; and the river, when it received it, would naturally bear it away and disperse it. Thus is this lake said to have been dug out.

Now the twelve kings continued to rule justly, but in course of time it happened thus:--After sacrifice in the temple of Hephaistos they were about to make libation on the last day of the feast, and the chief-priest, in bringing out for them the golden cups with which they had been wont to pour libations, missed his reckoning and brought eleven only for the twelve kings. Then that one of them who was standing last in order, namely Psammetichos, since he had no cup took off from his head his helmet, which was of bronze, and having held it out to receive the wine he proceeded to make libation: likewise all the other kings were wont to wear helmets and they happened to have them then. Now Psammetichos held out his helmet with no treacherous meaning; but they taking note of that which had been done by Psammetichos and of the oracle, namely how it had been declared to them that whosoever of them should make libation with a bronze cup should be sole king of Egypt, recollecting, I say, the saying of the Oracle, they did not indeed deem it right to slay Psammetichos, since they found by examination that he had not done it with any forethought, but they determined to strip him of almost all his power and to drive him away into the fen-country, and that from the fen- country he should not hold any dealings with the rest of Egypt. This Psammetichos had formerly been a fugitive from the Ethiopian Sabacos who had killed his father Necos, from him, I say, he had then been a fugitive in Syria; and when the Ethiopian had departed in consequence of the vision of the dream, the Egyptians who were of the district of Sais brought him back to his own country. Then afterwards, when he was king, it was his fate to be a fugitive a second time on account of the helmet, being driven by the eleven kings into the fen-country. So then holding that he had been grievously wronged by them, he thought how he might take vengeance on those who had driven him out: and when he had sent to the Oracle of Leto in the city of Buto, where the Egyptians have their most truthful Oracle, there was given to him the reply that vengeance would come when men of bronze appeared from the sea. And he was strongly disposed not to believe that bronze men would come to help him; but after no long time had passed, certain Ionians and Carians who had sailed forth for plunder were compelled to come to shore in Egypt, and they having landed and being clad in bronze armour, came to the fen-land and brought a report to Psammetichos that bronze men had come from the sea and were plundering the plain. So he, perceiving that the saying of the Oracle was coming to pass, dealt in a friendly manner with the Ionians and Carians, and with large promises he persuaded them to take his part. Then when he had persuaded them, with the help of those Egyptians who favoured his cause and of these foreign mercenaries he overthrew the kings. Having thus got power over all Egypt, Psammetichos made for Hephaistos that gateway of the temple at Memphis which is turned towards the South Wind; and he built a court for Apis, in which Apis is kept when he appears, opposite to the gateway of the temple, surrounded all with pillars and covered with figures; and instead of columns there stand to support the roof of the court colossal statues twelve cubits high. Now Apis is in the tongue of the Hellenes Epaphos. To the Ionians and to the Carians who had helped him Psammetichos granted portions of land to dwell in, opposite to one another with the river Nile between, and these were called "Encampments"; these portions of land he gave them, and he paid them besides all that he had promised: moreover he placed with them Egyptian boys to have them taught the Hellenic tongue; and from these, who learnt the language thoroughly, are descended the present class of interpreters in Egypt. Now the Ionians and Carians occupied these portions of land for a long time, and they are towards the sea a little below the city of Bubastis, on that which is called the Pelusian mouth of the Nile. These men king Amasis afterwards removed from thence and established them at Memphis, making them into a guard for himself against the Egyptians: and they being settled in Egypt, we who are Hellenes know by intercourse with them the certainty of all that which happened in Egypt beginning from king Psammetichos and afterwards; for these were the first men of foreign tongue who settled in Egypt: and in the land from which they were removed there still remained down to my time the sheds where their ships were drawn up and the ruins of their houses.

Thus then Psammetichos obtained Egypt: and of the Oracle which is in Egypt I have made mention often before this, and now I give an account of it, seeing that it is worthy to be described. This Oracle which is in Egypt is sacred to Leto, and it is established in a great city near that mouth of the Nile which is called Sebennytic, as one sails up the river from the sea; and the name of this city where the Oracle is found is Buto, as I have said before in mentioning it. In this Buto there is a temple of Apollo and Artemis; and the temple-house of Leto, in which the Oracle is, is both great in itself and has a gateway of the height of ten fathoms: but that which caused me most to marvel of the things to be seen there, I will now tell. There is in this sacred enclosure a house of Leto made of one single stone upon the top, the cornice measuring four cubits. This house then of all the things that were to be seen by me in that temple is the most marvellous, and among those which come next is the island called Chemmis. This is situated in a deep and broad lake by the side of the temple at Buto, and it is said by the Egyptians that this island is a floating island. I myself did not see it either floating about or moved from its place, and I feel surprise at hearing of it, wondering if it be indeed a floating island. In this island of which I speak there is a great temple-house of Apollo, and three several altars are set up within, and there are planted in the island many palm-trees and other trees, both bearing fruit and not bearing fruit. And the Egyptians, when they say that it is floating, add this story, namely that in this island which formerly was not floating, Leto, being one of the eight gods who came into existence first, and dwelling in the city of Buto where she has this Oracle, received Apollo from Isis as a charge and preserved him, concealing him in the island which is said now to be a floating island, at that time when Typhon

65

came after him seeking everywhere and desiring to find the son of Osiris. Now they say that Apollo and Artemis are children of Dionysos and of Isis, and that Leto became their nurse and preserver; and in the Egyptian tongue Apollo is Oros, Demeter is Isis, and Artemis is Bubastis. From this story and from no other AEschylus the son of Euphorion took this which I shall say, wherein he differs from all the preceding poets; he represented namely that Artemis was the daughter of Demeter. For this reason then, they say, it became a floating island.

Such is the story which they tell; but as for Psammetichos, he was king over Egypt for four-and-fifty years, of which for thirty years save one he was sitting before Azotos, a great city of Syria, besieging it, until at last he took it: and this Azotos of all cities about which we have knowledge held out for the longest time under a siege.

The son of Psammetichos was Necos, and he became king of Egypt. This man was the first who attempted the channel leading to the Erythraian Sea, which Dareios the Persian afterwards completed: the length of this is a voyage of four days, and in breadth it was so dug that two triremes could go side by side driven by oars; and the water is brought into it from the Nile. The channel is conducted a little above the city of Bubastis by Patumos the Arabian city, and runs into the Erythraian Sea: and it is dug first along those parts of the plain of Egypt which lie towards Arabia, just above which run the mountains which extend opposite Memphis, where are the stone-quarries,--along the base of these mountains the channel is conducted from West to East for a great way; and after that it is directed towards a break in the hills and tends from these mountains towards the noon-day and the South Wind to the Arabian gulf. Now in the place where the journey is least and shortest from the Northern to the Southern Sea (which is also called Erythraian), that is from Mount Casion, which is the boundary between Egypt and Syria, the distance is exactly a thousand furlongs to the Arabian gulf; but the channel is much longer, since it is more winding; and in the reign of Necos there perished while digging it twelve myriads of the Egyptians. Now Necos ceased in the midst of his digging, because the utterance of an Oracle impeded him, which was to the effect that he was working for the Barbarian: and the Egyptians call all men Barbarians who do not agree with them in speech. Thus having ceased from the work of the channel, Necos betook himself to raging wars, and triremes were built by him, some for the Northern Sea and others in the Arabian gulf for the Erythraian Sea; and of these the sheds are still to be seen. These ships he used when he needed them; and also on land Necos engaged battle at Magdolos with the Syrians, and conquered them; and after this he took Cadytis, which is a great city of Syria: and the dress which he wore when he made these conquests he dedicated to Apollo, sending it to Branchidai of the Milesians. After this, having reigned in all sixteen years, he brought his life to an end, and handed on the kingdom to Psammis his son.

While this Psammis was king of Egypt, there came to him men sent by the Eleians, who boasted that they ordered the contest at Olympia in the most just and honourable manner possible and thought that not even the Egyptians, the wisest of men, could find out anything besides, to be added to their rules. Now when the Eleians came to Egypt and said that for which they had come, then this king called together those of the Egyptians who were reputed the wisest, and when the Egyptians had come together they heard the Eleians tell of all that which it was their part to do in regard to the contest; and when they had related everything, they said that they had come to learn in addition anything which the Egyptians might be able to find out besides, which was juster than this. They then having consulted together asked the Eleians whether their own citizens took part in the contest; and they said that it was permitted to any one who desired it, to take part in the contest: upon which the Egyptians said that in so ordering the games they had wholly missed the mark of justice; for it could not be but that they would take part with the man of their own State, if he was contending, and so act unfairly to the stranger: but if they really desired, as they said, to order the games justly, and if this was the cause for which they had come to Egypt, they advised them to order the contest so as to be for strangers alone to contend in, and that no Eleian should be permitted to contend. Such was the suggestion made by the Egyptians to the Eleians.

When Psammis had been king of Egypt for only six years and had made an expedition to Ethiopia and immediately afterwards had ended his life, Apries the son of Psammis received the kingdom in succession. This man came to be the most prosperous of all the kings up to that time except only his forefather Psammetichos; and he reigned five-and-twenty years, during which he led an army against Sidon and fought a sea- fight with the king of Tyre. Since however it was fated that evil should come upon him it came by occasion of a matter which I shall relate at greater length in the Libyan history, and at present but shortly. Apries having sent a great expedition against the Kyrenians, met with correspondingly great disaster; and the Egyptians considering him to blame for this revolted from him, supposing that Apries had with forethought sent them out to evident calamity, in order (as they said) that there might be a slaughter of them, and he might the more securely rule over the other Egyptians. Being indignant at this, both these men who had returned from the expedition and also the friends of those who had perished made revolt openly. Hearing this Apries sent to them Amasis, to cause them to cease by persuasion; and when he had come and was seeking to restrain the Egyptians, as he was speaking and telling them not to do so, one of the Egyptians stood up behind him and put a helmet upon his head, saying as he did so that he put it on to crown him king. And to him this that was done was in some degree not unwelcome, as he proved by his behaviour; for as soon as the revolted Egyptians had set him up as king, he prepared to march against Apries: and Apries hearing this sent to Amasis one of the Egyptians who were about his own person, a man of reputation, whose name was Patarbemis, enjoining him to bring Amasis alive into his presence. When this Patarbemis came and summoned Amasis, the latter, who happened to be sitting on horseback, lifted up his leg and behaved in an unseemly manner, bidding him take that back to Apries. Nevertheless, they say, Patarbemis made demand of him that he should go to the king, seeing that the king had sent to summon him; and he answered him that he had for some time past been preparing to do so, and that Apries would have no occasion to find fault with him, for he would both come himself and bring others with him. Then Patarbemis both perceiving his intention from that which he said, and also seeing his preparations, departed in haste, desiring to make known as quickly as possible to the king the things which were being done: and when he came back to Apries not bringing Amasis, the king paying no regard to that which he said, but being moved by violent anger, ordered his ears and his nose to be cut off. And the rest of the Egyptians who still remained on his side, when they saw the man of most repute among them thus suffering shameful outrage, waited no longer but joined the others in revolt, and delivered themselves over to Amasis. Then Apries having heard this also, armed his foreign mercenaries and marched against the Egyptians: now he had about him Carian and Ionian mercenaries to the number of thirty thousand; and his royal palace was in the city of Sais, of great size and worthy to be seen. So Apries and his army were going against the Egyptians, and Amasis and those with him were going against the mercenaries; and both sides came to the city of Momemphis and were about to make trial of one another in fight.

Now of the Egyptians there are seven classes, and of these one class is called that of the priests, and another that of the warriors, while the others are the cowherds, swineherds, shopkeepers, interpreters, and boatmen. This is the number of the classes of the Egyptians, and their names are given them from the occupations which they follow. Of them the warriors are called Calasirians and Hermotybians, and they are of the following districts,--for all Egypt is divided into districts. The districts of the Hermotybians are those of Busiris, Sais, Chemmis, Papremis, the island called Prosopitis, and the half of Natho,--of these districts are the Hermotybians, who reached when most numerous the number of sixteen myriads. Of these not one has been learnt anything of handicraft, but they are given up to war entirely. Again the districts of the Calasirians are those of Thebes, Bubastis, Aphthis, Tanis, Mendes, Sebennytos, Athribis, Pharbaithos, Thmuis, Onuphis, Anytis, Myecphoris,--this last is on an island opposite to the city of Bubastis. These are the districts of the Calasirians; and they reached, when most numerous, to the number of five-and-twenty myriads of men; nor is it lawful for these, any more than for the others, to practise any craft; but they practise that which has to do with war only, handing down the tradition from father to son. Now whether the Hellenes have learnt this also from the Egyptians, I am not able to say for certain, since I see that the Thracians also and Scythians and Persians and Lydians and almost all the Barbarians esteem those of their citizens who learn the arts, and the descendants of them, as less honourable than the rest; while those who have got free from all practice of manual arts are accounted noble, and especially those who are devoted to war: however that may be, the Hellenes have all learnt this, and especially the Lacedemonians; but the Corinthians least of all cast slight upon those who practise handicraft.

The following privilege was specially granted to this class and to none others of the Egyptians except the priests, that is to say, each man had twelve yokes of land specially granted to him free from imposts: now the yoke of land measures a hundred Egyptian cubits every way, and the Egyptian cubit is, as it happens, equal to that of Samos. This, I say, was a special privilege granted to all, and they also had certain advantages in turn and not the same men twice; that is to say, a thousand of the Calasirians and a thousand of the Hermotybians acted as body-guard to the king during each year; and these had besides their yokes of land an allowance given them for each day of five pounds weight of bread to each man, and two pounds of beef, and four half-pints of wine. This was the allowance given to those who were serving as the king's body-guard for the time being.

So when Apries leading his foreign mercenaries, and Amasis at the head of the whole body of the Egyptians, in their approach to one another had come to the city of Momemphis, they engaged in battle: and although the foreign troops fought well, yet being much inferior in number they were worsted by reason of this. But Apries is said to have supposed that not even a god would be able to cause him to cease from his rule, so firmly did he think that it was established. In that battle then, I say, he was worsted, and being taken alive was brought away to the city of Sais, to that which had formerly been his own dwelling but from thenceforth was the palace of Amasis. There for some time he was kept in the palace, and Amasis dealt well with him but at last, since the Egyptians blamed him, saying that he acted not rightly in keeping alive him who was the greatest foe both to themselves and to him, therefore he delivered Apries over to the Egyptians; and they strangled him, and after that buried him in the burial-place of his fathers: this is in the temple of Athene, close to the sanctuary, on the left hand as you enter. Now the men of Sais buried all those of this district who had been kings, within the temple; for the tomb of Amasis also, though it is further from the sanctuary than that of Apries and his forefathers, yet this too is within the court of the temple, and it consists of a colonnade of stone of great size, with pillars carved to imitate date-palms, and otherwise sumptuously adorned; and within the colonnade are double doors, and inside the doors a sepulchral chamber. Also at Sais there is the burial-place of him whom I account it not pious to name in connexion with such a matter, which is in the temple of Athene behind the house of the goddess, stretching along the whole wall of it; and in the sacred enclosure stand great obelisks of stone, and near them is a lake adorned with an edging of stone and fairly made in a circle, being in size, as it seemed to me, equal to that which is called the "Round Pool" in Delos. On this lake they perform by night the show of his sufferings, and this the Egyptians call Mysteries. Of these things I know more fully in detail how they take place, but I shall leave this unspoken; and of the mystic rites of Demeter, which the Hellenes call /thesmophoria/, of these also, although I know, I shall leave unspoken all except so much as piety permits me to tell. The daughters of Danaos were they who brought this rite out of Egypt and taught it to the women of the Pelasgians; then afterwards when all the inhabitants of Peloponnese were driven out by the Dorians, the rite was lost, and only those who were left behind of the Peloponnesians and not driven out, that is to say the Arcadians, preserved it.

Apries having thus been overthrown, Amasis became king, being of the district of Sais, and the name of the city whence he was is Siuph. Now at the first the Egyptians despised Amasis and held him in no great regard, because he had been a man of the people and was of no distinguished family; but afterwards Amasis won them over to himself by wisdom and not wilfulness. Among innumerable other things of price which he had, there was a foot-basin of gold in which both Amasis himself and all his guests were wont always to wash their feet. This he broke up, and of it he caused to be made the image of a god, and set it up in the city, where it was most convenient; and the Egyptians went continually to visit the image and did great reverence to it. Then Amasis, having learnt that which was done by the men of the city, called together the Egyptians and made known to them the matter, saying that the image had been produced from the foot-basin, into which formerly the Egyptians used to vomit and make water, and in which they washed their feet, whereas now they did to it great reverence; and just so, he continued, had he himself now fared, as the foot-basin; for though formerly he was a man of the people, yet now he was their king, and he bade them accordingly honour him and have regard for him. In such manner he won the Egyptians to himself, so that they consented to be his subjects; and his ordering of affairs was this:--In the early morning, and until the time of the filling of the market he did with a good will the business which was brought before him; but after this he passed the time in drinking and in jesting at his boon-companions, and was frivolous and playful. And his friends being troubled at it admonished him in some such words as these: "O king, thou dost not rightly govern thyself in thus letting thyself descend to behaviour so trifling; for thou oughtest rather to have been sitting throughout the day stately upon a stately throne and administering thy business; and so the Egyptians would have been assured that they were ruled by a great man, and thou wouldest have had a better report: but as it is, thou art acting by no means in a kingly fashion." And he answered them thus: "They who have bows stretch them at such time as they wish to use them, and when they have finished using them they loose them again; for if they were stretched tight always they would break, so that the men would not be able to use them when they needed them. So also is the state of man: if he should always be in earnest and not relax himself for sport at the due time, he would either go mad or be struck with stupor before he was aware; and knowing this well, I distribute a portion of the time to each of the two ways of living." Thus he replied to his friends. It is said however that Amasis, even when he was in a private station, was a lover of drinking and of jesting, and not at all seriously disposed; and whenever his means of livelihood failed him through his drinking and luxurious living, he would go about and steal; and they from whom he stole would charge him with having their property, and when he denied it would bring him before the judgment of an Oracle, whenever there was one in their place; and many times he was convicted by the Oracles and many times he was absolved: and then when finally he became king he did as follows:--as many of the gods as had absolved him and pronounced him not to be a thief, to their temples he paid no regard, nor gave anything for the further adornment of them, nor even visited them to offer sacrifice, considering them to be worth nothing and to possess lying Oracles; but as many as had convicted him of being a thief, to these he paid very great regard, considering them to be truly gods, and to present Oracles which did not lie. First in Sais he built and completed for Athene a temple-gateway which is a great marvel, and he far surpassed herein all who had done the like before, both in regard to height and greatness, so large are the stones and of such quality. Then secondly he dedicated great colossal statues and man-headed sphinxes very large, and for restoration he caused to be brought from the stone-quarries which are opposite Memphis, others of very great size from the city of Elephantine, distant a voyage of not less than twenty days from Sais: and of them all I marvel most at this, namely a monolith chamber which he brought from the city of Elephantine; and they were three years engaged in bringing this, and two thousand men were appointed to convey it, who all were of the class of boatmen. Of this house the length outside is one-and-twenty cubits, the breadth is fourteen cubits, and the height eight. These are the measures of the monolith house outside; but the length inside is eighteen cubits and five-sixths of a cubit, the breadth twelve cubits, and the height five cubits. This lies by the side of the entrance to the temple; for within the temple they did not draw it, because, as it is said, while the house was being drawn along, the chief artificer of it groaned aloud, seeing that much time had been spent and he was wearied by the work; and Amasis took it to heart as a warning and did not allow them to draw it further onwards. Some say on the other hand that a man was killed by it, of those who were heaving it with levers, and that it was not drawn in for that reason. Amasis also dedicated in all the other temples which were of repute, works which are worth seeing for their size, and among them also at Memphis the colossal statue which lies on its back in front of the temple of Hephaistos, whose length is five-and-seventy feet; and on the same base made of the same stone are set two colossal statues, each of twenty feet in length, one on this side and the other on that side of the large statue. There is also another of stone of the same size in Sais, lying in the same manner as that at Memphis. Moreover Amasis was he who built and finished for Isis her temple at Memphis, which is of great size and very worthy to be seen.

In the reign of Amasis it is said that Egypt became more prosperous than at any other time before, both in regard to that which comes to the land from the river and in regard to that which comes from the land to its inhabitants, and that at this time the inhabited towns in it numbered in all twenty thousand.

It was Amasis too who established the law that every year each one of the Egyptians should declare to the ruler of his district, from what source he got his livelihood, and if any man did not do this or did not make declaration of an honest way of living, he should be punished with death. Now Solon the Athenian received from Egypt this law and had it enacted for the Athenians, and they have continued to observe it, since it is a law with which none can find fault.

Moreover Amasis became a lover of the Hellenes; and besides other proofs of friendship which he gave to several among them, he also granted the city of Naucratis for those of them who came to Egypt to dwell in; and to those who did not desire to stay, but who made voyages thither, he granted portions of land to set up altars and make sacred enclosures for their gods. Their greatest enclosure and that one which has most name and is most frequented is called the Hellenion, and this was established by the following cities in common: --of the Ionians Chios, Teos, Phocaia, Clazomenai, of the Dorians Rhodes, Cnidos, Halicarnassos, Phaselis, and of the Aiolians Mytilene alone. To these belongs this enclosure and these are the cities which appoint superintendents of the port; and all other cities which claim a share in it, are making a claim without any right. Besides this the Eginetans established on their own account a sacred enclosure dedicated to Zeus, the Samians one to Hera, and the Milesians one to Apollo. Now in old times Naucratis alone was an open trading-place, and no other place in Egypt: and if any one came to any other of the Nile mouths, he was compelled to swear that he came not thither of his own free will, and when he had thus sworn his innocence

he had to sail with his ship to the Canobic mouth, or if it were not possible to sail by reason of contrary winds, then he had to carry his cargo round the head of the Delta in boats to Naucratis: thus highly was Naucratis privileged. Moreover when the Amphictyons had let out the contract for building the temple which now exists at Delphi, agreeing to pay a sum of three hundred talents (for the temple which formerly stood there had been burnt down of itself), it fell to the share of the people of Delphi to provide the fourth part of the payment;
and accordingly the Delphians went about to various cities and collected contributions. And when they did this they got from Egypt as much as from any place, for Amasis gave them a thousand talents' weight of alum, while the Hellenes who dwelt in Egypt gave them twenty pounds of silver.

Also with the people of Kyrene Amasis made an agreement for friendship and alliance; and he resolved too to marry a wife from thence, whether because he desired to have a wife of Hellenic race, or, apart from that, on account of friendship for the people of Kyrene: however that may be, he married, some say the daughter of Battos, others of Arkesilaos, and others of Critobulos, a man of repute among the citizens; and her name was Ladike. Now whenever Amasis lay with her he found himself unable to have intercourse, but with his other wives he associated as he was wont; and as this happened repeatedly, Amasis said to his wife, whose name was Ladike: "Woman, thou hast given me drugs, and thou shall surely perish more miserably than any other." Then Ladike, when by her denials Amasis was not at all appeased in his anger against her, made a vow in her soul to Aphrodite, that if Amasis on that night had intercourse with her (seeing that this was the remedy for her danger), she would send an image to be dedicated to her at Kyrene; and after the vow immediately Amasis had intercourse, and from thenceforth whenever Amasis came in to her he had intercourse with her; and after this he became very greatly attached to her. And Ladike paid the vow that she had made to the goddess; for she had an image made and sent it to Kyrene, and it is still preserved even to my own time, standing with its face turned away from the city of the Kyrenians. This Ladike Cambyses, having conquered Egypt and heard from her who she was, sent back unharmed to Kyrene.

Amasis also dedicated offerings in Hellas, first at Kyrene an image of Athene covered over with gold and a figure of himself made like by painting; then in the temple of Athene at Lindos two images of stone and a corslet of linen worthy to be seen; and also at Samos two wooden figures of himself dedicated to Hera, which were standing even to my own time in the great temple, behind the doors. Now at Samos he dedicated offerings because of the guest-friendship between himself and Polycrates the son of Aiakes; at Lindos for no guest-friendship but because the temple of Athene at Lindos is said to have been founded by the daughters of Danaos, who had touched land there at the time when they were fleeing from the sons of Aigyptos. These offerings were dedicated by Amasis; and he was the first of men who conquered Cyprus and subdued it so that it paid him tribute.

Printed in the United States
140510LV00002B/1/A